ELECTRIC BREAD®
The Simple Solution to Bread Machine Success

As the established classic and industry leader, *Electric Bread* offers 160 pages of proven recipes for breads, specialty doughs and spreads. Clear guidance on ingredients and troubleshooting, and a mini-catalog of useful accessories make it a valuable addition to the home bread bakery.

The "secret ingredient" is the on-going research at the bustling Innovative Cooking Enterprises' test kitchen. The ever-current information ensures quality *Electric Bread* loaves with the bread machine of your choice.

Full page photos join with an easy, understandable narrative to make this gourmet recipe book as user friendly as the push-button bread machines themselves!

D0288387

BREAD®
electric

Innovative Cooking Enterprises

I.C.E. Inc. Anchorage, Alaska

Developed by:
Innovative Cooking Enterprises * I.C.E., Inc.

Cover, Book Design & Photography by:
Art & International Productions
Sasha Sagan & Jim Tilly

Written by:
Suzan Nightingale

ELECTRIC BREAD is a registered trademark of
Innovative Cooking Enterprises * I.C.E., Inc.

Published by Innovative Cooking Enterprises * I.C.E., Inc.
P. O. Box 240888
Anchorage, Alaska 99524-0888

SAN 297-441X

First Paperback Printing, September, 1994

Printed in China

Library of Congress Catalog Card Number: 91-72650

ISBN 0-9629831-5-2

Table of Contents

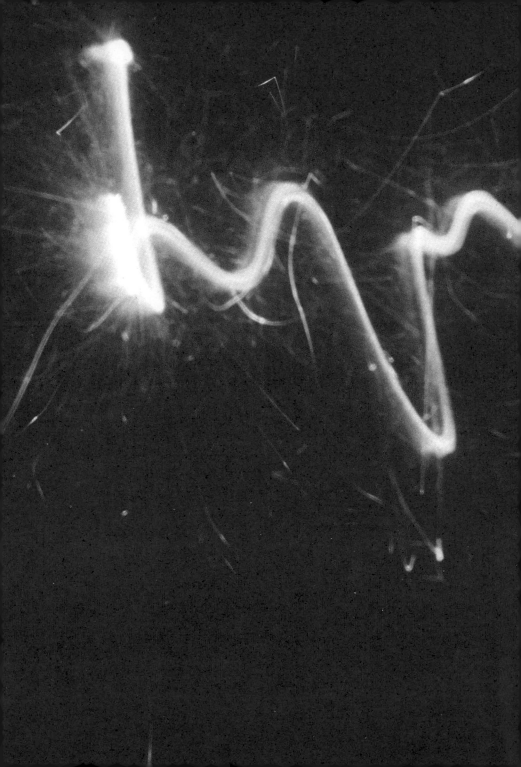

ELECTRIC BREAD,
YOUR MACHINE
& INGREDIENTS

Welcome to ELECTRIC BREAD -
recipes for people with more taste
than time. We baked over 10,000
loaves to ensure our recipes work in
<u>every</u> bread machine model, and made
some important discoveries along the
way. Come into our kitchen...
and we'll tell you what we've learned.

Every chef has a secret ingredient, and we'll tell you ours — our test kitchen. With more than 80 bread machines humming around the clock, ours is the only kitchen working directly with every machine manufacturer and major flour and yeast producer. Our on-going research ensures that *ELECTRIC BREAD* keeps abreast of the latest developments in technology and ingredients.

But before the research, our test kitchen began with bread machine owners like you.

ELECTRIC BREAD was born of enthusiasm — and frustration. All of us own home bread machines and, like you, we lead busy lives.

We wanted new and interesting recipes that really worked. We wanted to know what other doughy delights we could make in our machines. And we wanted recipes that worked in *every* make and model owned by our friends.

The secret of our success - the Test Kitchen working with new bread machines, flour and yeast to ensure our information is up to date.

Maybe it was the long Alaskan winter. Or maybe it was our conviction that quality, innovative breads *weren't* too much to ask from these incredible machines. After searching in vain, we decided to open our own test kitchen and write our own recipe book.

Our goal was simple: every recipe had to produce *quality bread* in every model on the market. No doorstops, no fluffy exploding loaves, no toasted cardboard — quality bread every time.

And we've done it! 10,000 loaves later, we've found that bread machines are both demanding *and* forgiving. They require precise measurement and careful attention to detail. Yet they're so consistent, so easy, and so fun, they beg you to come out and play.

OUR RECIPES HAVE BEEN TESTED IN THESE MACHINES:

American Harvest • Betty Crocker • Black & Decker • Breadman
Chefmate • Charlescraft • Circulair • Citizen • Dak • Decosonic
Goldstar • Hitachi • Kenmore • Magic Mill • Maxim • Mister Loaf
National • Oster • Panasonic • Regal • Sanyo • Singer • Toastmaster
Welbilt • West Bend • Zojirushi

TIPS
FOR SUCCESS

Each recipe contains specific hints. These tips apply to every machine and recipe.

MEASURING

Bread machines don't ask much of the home baker, but they do require one thing: precision. Careful measurements can make the difference between a luscious loaf and a disappointing dud. Scoop dry ingredients into a regulation measuring cup and tap lightly to make sure contents are settled. Make certain the top is level - a heaping cup can be a cup-and-a-half if you're not careful. We use clear measuring cups for liquids. Set the cup on a counter and check at eye level to make sure you're on the mark. Tableware doesn't cut it when accuracy counts. Key ingredients - like yeast, salt and sugar - use small exact quantities. So use standard measuring spoons with ingredients levelled off.

RECIPE SIZE

The recipe size for you depends on your machine. Different bread machines have different pan capacities. Each *Electric Bread* recipe gives ingredients for a regular and a large loaf.   With a liquid measuring cup, determine how many cups of water your pan holds when filled to the rim. Then use the tested recipe size shown below for your pan capacity.

Pan Capacity	Recipe Size
Less than 12 cups	Regular
12 to 16 cups	Large
More than 16 cups	Double Regular

EXTRA KNEAD

We developed the "extra knead" technique to give bread structure, and to make French bread, whole wheat and pumpernickel. Simply start your machine and let it go through the first knead, then stop and restart it from the beginning again. For even lighter results using heavier flours, allow the dough to rise before restarting your machine. Some newer models feature a whole wheat or French cycle. These cycles may replace the double knead used in some of our recipes.

WATER TEMPERATURE

Use tepid water in your machine. Cold water won't activate the yeast, hot water will speed it too much, and very hot water will kill it.

LOADING YOUR MACHINE

Load ingredients in the order suggested in your owner's manual. For consistency's sake, all of our recipes are listed with water first and yeast last. Because the liquid activates the yeast, you don't want your yeast contacting the water ahead of time - especially on a delayed time

bake. Load dried fruits, vegetables and spices away from liquid ingredients so they don't soak up water and sabotage the liquid/ flour ratio. For the best results, use our recipes with your own machine's procedures.

SPOILAGE

Store yeast in a cool, dry, airtight container. Each yeast has its own shelf life, but once opened, all yeast should be stored in the refrigerator. Never use perishable ingredients - milk, yogurt, meat, cheese, eggs - in a delayed time-bake cycle. Left unrefrigerated, they can spoil before the baking process even starts.

FRUIT

Always drain canned fruits to keep an accurate liquid/flour ratio. When using dried fruit, remember that older fruit has a more concentrated sugar content; too much may overactivate the yeast. Beware of fruit (such as apricots) treated with sulfur dioxide; this preservative can kill the yeast.

FLOUR SELECTION

Shop for good bread flour. Most all-purpose flours don't have enough protein to produce quality bread. Because flour depends on the wheat crop, its moisture and protein content vary from year to year. This may affect the performance of some of your favorite recipes, as will changing flour brands.

LOAF SIZE AND TEXTURE

One of the most frequent comments we receive on our customer service line is: "My bread didn't turn out right." Many have wrestled with disappointment over a loaf's appearance only to find out later that it wasn't a failure at all, and their loaf was supposed to be that way.

Different kinds of bread have different textures and heights because they are made of different ingredients. Our Pumpernickel recipe, for example, produces a shorter, denser loaf than Saffron. As a general rule, whole wheat flours produce a denser loaf than lighter flours. Some people like a chewier texture for sandwiches, others want their sandwiches light and fluffy.

Comparative Loaf Size
Saffron (left) and Pumpernickel

Because different people like different bread, the guide on the following page indicates the *relative* size and texture of our *Electric Bread* recipes. Each recipe has a relative rating between 1 and 5. Pumpernickel (with a rating of 1) is a smaller, compact loaf with a denser texture. Saffron (with a rating of 5) is a large, light, airy loaf with a delicate texture.

As you can see, *Electric Bread* brings you a wide range of variety. Use the Loaf Size and Texture Guide on the next page to evaluate your loaf results or to select recipes with the texture you prefer.

Comparative Loaf Texture
Pumpernickel (left) and Saffron

NUTRITIONAL INFORMATION

For the nutrition conscious baker, each recipe provides calories, cholesterol and sodium content and the percentage of protein, carbohydrates and fat. *Electric Bread* nutritional information is based on 8 servings per regular loaf, 12 servings for a large loaf and 16 servings for a double-regular loaf.

LOAF SIZE & TEXTURE GUIDE

Bread Recipe & Page Number	1	2	3	4	5
Almond Poppy, 52				X	
Apple Oat, 42				X	
Apricot, 86				X	
Baked Potato, 76			X		
Banana Granola, 118		X			
Bits o' Bacon, 72				X	
Bleu Cheese & Port, 114				X	
Cajun Spice, 50				X	
Carrot, 68			X		
Certainly Citrus, 46			X		
Challah, 82					X
Cherry Yogurt, 24					X
Chocolate Cherry, 104		X			
Cinco de Mayo, 22				X	
Classic White, 26				X	
Cottage Dill, 48				X	
100% Crunch, 78	X				
Easy French, 62		X			
Fall Harvest, 106				X	
Garden Herb, 80				X	
Garlic, 56		X			
Greek Isle, 110				X	
Health Grain, 20				X	
Honey Mustard, 40			X		
Honey Wheat, 54				X	
Italian Wheat, 70				X	

Bread Recipe & Page Number	1	2	3	4	5
Kulich, 36				X	
Light Rye, 64	X				
Luscious Luau, 94				X	
Maraschino Pecan, 60				X	
Mocha Java, 84				X	
Multi-Grain & More, 38			X		
Nutty Coconut, 100				X	
Onion, 90				X	
Outrageously Oatmeal, 102				X	
Peaches & Cream, 98				X	
Peanut Butter, 44				X	
Pizza Pleasure, 96				X	
Pumpernickel, 88	X				
Raisin Bread, 28				X	
Rum Raisin, 92				X	
Saffron, 58				X	
Saucy Apple, 74	X				
Sourdough White, 116				X	
Sun Nut, 112				X	
Swedish Limpa, 32			X		
Sweet Coconut Curry, 66				X	
Tabouli, 108				X	
Tangy Cranberry, 120	X				
Tropical Medley, 34		X			
100% Whole Wheat, 30			X		

This chart gives a relative rating, ranging from 1 to 5, for each *Electric Bread* recipe. The number 1 indicates the densest loaves and 5 the lightest.

Our executive chef, Greg, likes to say that cooking is an art but baking is a science. He doesn't mean you have to be Einstein to bake bread, just that basic chemistry is what turns flour and yeast into bread.

The ingredients work off one another in a precise way, and slight mismeasurements - or inappropriate ingredients - can throw off that critical balance.

Flour, for instance, isn't just "flour" anymore. Different flours are made from particular wheats for distinct uses, and they produce dramatically different results in home bakeries. Pastry, cake and many all-purpose flours don't work with yeast the way bread flour does. A loaf made from all white bread flour will be much taller than a 100% whole wheat loaf.

Good bread flours include hard wheats that have the high protein/high gluten content needed to give the bread structure. Take the time to cruise the flour aisles in your markets, read some labels, and note the products that specify they are formulated especially for bread.

One of the great things about home bakeries is that you don't need a Ph.D. in Yeast to make quality bread. The machines conquer the mystique of yeast with the push of a button. Still, a short explanation will help take the mystery out of what's going on under that closed lid.

Yeast is a living organism. Mixed with water and sugar, the yeast wakes up during the kneading process and gives off carbon dioxide bubbles, filling your bread with tiny holes that make it rise. That's why a high protein, high gluten flour is important; the gluten is what works with the gas to achieve the right structure.

Most recipes contain sugar in some form - not for sweetness but to jump-start the yeast and to promote browning. Salt, on the other hand, inhibits the yeast, but is needed for flavor - a balance to keep in mind as you experiment with sugary fruits or salty meats in your bread machine.

Because bread is the result of this chemical reaction, *precise measurements are vital.* Grandma may have been able to eyeball her flour, but bread machines are designed for consistently measured ingredients.

In the following pages, we talk about some of the ingredients we used in our test kitchen. But remember, geographic regions often have different brands and sometimes their own regional mills. It's worth the investment for you to buy several types and experiment with your own machine, comparing loaf height, texture and taste from the same basic recipe. If you bake several loaves back-to-back, you'll spot the differences.

flour

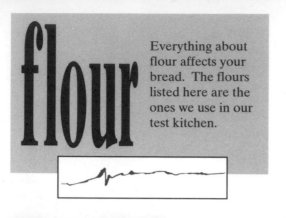

Everything about flour affects your bread. The flours listed here are the ones we use in our test kitchen.

GOLD MEDAL - General Mills provides a variety of flour products from hard and soft wheats. Widely available, Gold Medal's Better for Bread Flour is blended from a selection of high protein flours. It contains a small amount of ascorbic acid to produce better volume and crumb structure. Unbleached and unbromated, this finely milled flour produced a soft, airy bread with a crisp, flaky crust.

ARROWHEAD MILLS - Located on the high plains of the Texas Panhandle, Arrowhead Mills makes its all-natural flour from hard red winter wheat grown without insecticides or herbicides. Unbleached, this consistent performer baked a sturdy, flavorful loaf with a soft golden glow. Arrowhead Mills products are distributed nationwide.

BAKERS & CHEFS - For bakers looking for bread flour in larger quantities, Bakers & Chefs offers its enriched bleached bread flour in 25 lb. bags. Made from a blend of hard spring and winter wheat, Bakers & Chefs can be found at Sam's warehouse clubs.

ROBIN HOOD -These two flours were shipped to us from Canada where they are available nationwide. Made from a blend of Canadian spring, red winter and soft white wheats, Robin Hood produces a pleasant medium-weight loaf with the unique characteristic of a subtle, almost malt-like flavor.

PILLSBURY - Available nationwide, Pillsbury is known for the consistent quality of its baking products. Pillsbury's BEST Bread Flour is a finely milled flour that produces a light, fluffy loaf with a slight sweetness in taste. The Whole Wheat flour also produced a consistent flavorful loaf.

STONE-BUHR - This naturally aged whole-grain flour is ground slowly in old-fashioned stone mills. Both the unbleached white and whole wheat flours produced classically domed loaves with full-bodied texture, a crunchy crust and a whisper of sweetness. Made from high protein Montana hard red wheat, Stone-Buhr is available in 11 Western states.

The test kitchen also baked our recipes with a variety of other flours, including those manufactured by Five Roses of Canada, ConAgra, Dakota Mills, King Arthur and Hodgson Mills.

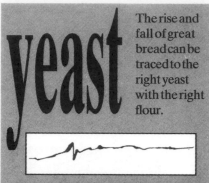

yeast

The rise and fall of great bread can be traced to the right yeast with the right flour.

If flour is the foundation of your bread, yeast is the primary building block. We used powdered yeasts - both the fast rise and the active dry - for their convenience and efficiency. Some yeasts enhance the flavor of your flour, while others impart a distinctive flavor of their own. And some yeasts work better with certain kinds of flours than others in bread machines. If you're using a heavier flour, and you want a lighter bread, try increasing the yeast by 1/8 teaspoon at a time.

BAKIPAN - This fast-rising yeast is available in Canada as Fermipan, and is being test marketed in the U.S. under the name of Bakipan. In our test loaves, it produced a uniform, springy texture. With no distracting yeast taste, Bakipan enhanced the natural flavor of the flour itself. Bakipan can be ordered by mail in the U.S. Call for information at (800) 665-0991.

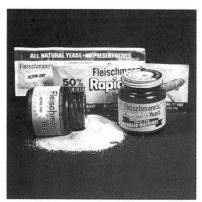

FLEISCHMANN'S - Widely available, Fleischmann's is known throughout the world of baking. Formulated in Active Dry and RapidRise varieties, it consistently produced a sturdy texture with uniform shape and air pocket distribution. We liked it best in the more complex breads with multiple ingredients and flavors.

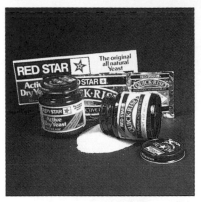

RED STAR - RED STAR Yeast & Products, a Division of Universal Foods Corporation, manufactures 100% all-natural RED STAR Active Dry and QUICK•RISE Yeasts. They are available in convenient packages or vacuum-packed jars. We like using RED STAR Yeast with light, finer milled flours.

SAF - Made in France, SAF's Instant Dry Baker's Yeast has long been a favorite of professional bakers. Its strength and forgiving nature make it ideal for home bakers, too. It was an instant favorite of our test kitchen staff because of its consistent performance and beautiful loaves. SAF is available in gourmet or specialty stores or by calling SAF at (800) 641-4615.

spices

Freshness and quality are key to premium flavor.

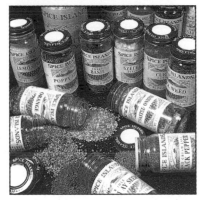

SPICE ISLANDS - Established in 1941, this is the only national brand of gourmet spices that grows herbs on its own farms in California in addition to importing select spices from around the world. Offering a high quality and complete gourmet seasoning assortment, Spice Islands is conveniently available at most grocery stores.

We also test with other spices and ingredients, including Morton & Bassett salt-free spices and Chef Paul Prudhomme's Magic Seasoning Blends' Seafood Magic, the flavorful fire in our Cajun Bread.

17

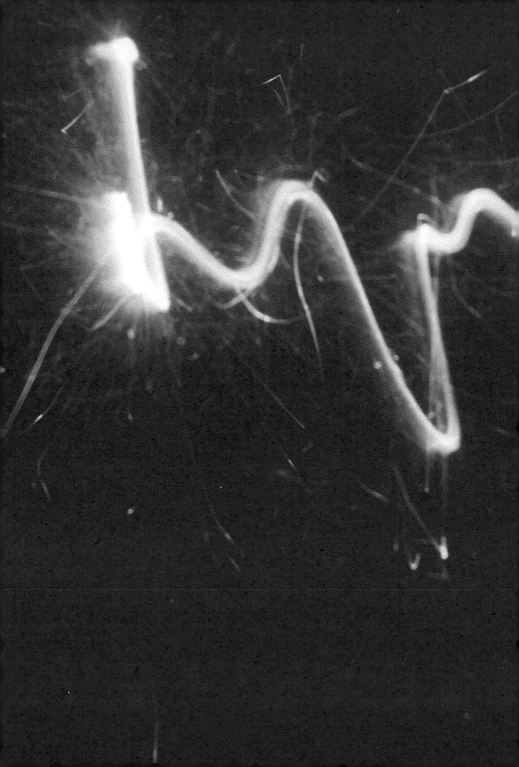

GOURMET BREADS

Man does not live by bread
alone - but you might try it
with our 51 gourmet recipes.
From the heartiest Health
Grain to the lightest
Luscious Luau, you'll find a
loaf for every occasion.
And best of all, they're
yours with the push of a
button!

Health Grain

Calories 173   Protein 12 %
Cholesterol .05 mg.   Carbohydrates 64 %
Sodium 243 mg.   Fat 24 %

Nutritional information per serving

Who said good health can't taste good? This bread has everything, including flavor. Moist with a light crunch, our Health Grain is chock full of good things. But you don't have to tell the finicky eaters about the bran or the wheat germ. Serve this with a fresh fruit plate, and let them think it's all about taste.

Success Hints

- If using the time bake cycle, place the carrots away from the yeast. This will help prevent the carrots from turning brown.

- This recipe can be used with the regular, rapid, or delayed time bake cycles.

regular loaf		large loaf
3/4 cup	**Water**	1 1/4 cups
1 1/2 cups	**White Bread Flour**	2 cups
1/4 cup	**Wheat Bread Flour**	3/4 cup
2 tsp.	**Dry Milk**	1 Tbsp.
1 tsp.	**Salt**	1 1/2 tsp.
2 tsp.	**Honey**	1 Tbsp.
1 Tbsp.	**Olive Oil**	2 Tbsp.
1/4 cup	**Carrots** chopped or grated	1/2 cup
1/4 cup	**Raisins**	1/2 cup
1/4 cup	**Sunflower Seeds**	1/2 cup
1/4 cup	**Bran Flakes**	1/2 cup
1 Tbsp.	**Wheat Germ**	2 Tbsp.
1 tsp.	**Yeast** fast rise	2 tsp.
	- or -	
2 tsp.	**Yeast** active dry	3 tsp.

Cinco de Mayo

Calories 131   Protein 12 %
Cholesterol 0 mg.   Carbohydrates 79 %
Sodium 174 mg.   Fat 9 %

Nutritional information per serving

Our Cinco de Mayo bread was inspired by Mexico's May 5th national holiday, but don't wait until then to try it! The jalapeño pepper and cilantro create a fiesta of flavor that's perfect for brisk fall weekends and cold winter nights. Served with chili, this lightly textured loaf will convince you never to go back to plain corn bread again. *Buen Apetito!*

Success Hints

- If you want a little more zip, increase jalapeño peppers to taste.

- Drain canned chilies and jalapeño peppers well. Be careful! Jalapeño and chili juice can sting. Be sure to wash your hands after preparation.

- This bread is a great party bread because of its unexpected texture and flavor.

- This recipe can be used with the regular and rapid bake cycles.

regular loaf		large loaf
2/3 cup	**Water**	1 cup
2 cups	**White Bread Flour**	3 cups
2 tsp.	**Sugar**	1 Tbsp.
1/2 tsp.	**Salt**	1 tsp.
2 tsp.	**Olive Oil**	1 Tbsp.
2/3 cup	**Corn Meal**	1 cup
1/3 cup	**Creamed Corn**	1/2 cup
2 Tbsp.	**Green Chilies** *canned/diced*	1/4 cup
1 tsp.	**Jalapeño Peppers** *canned/diced*	1/2 Tbsp.
1 tsp.	**Cilantro** *dried*	2 tsp.
1 1/2 tsp.	**Yeast** *fast rise*	2 tsp.
	- or -	
2 tsp.	**Yeast** *active dry*	3 tsp.

Cherry Yogurt

Calories 130   Protein 12 %
Cholesterol 0.30 mg.   Carbohydrates 86 %
Sodium 172 mg.   Fat 2 %

Nutritional information per serving

regular loaf		large loaf
1/2 cup	**Water**	3/4 cup
2 cups	**White Bread Flour**	3 cups
3/4 tsp.	**Salt**	1 1/4 tsp.
1/2 cup	**Cherries** *dried*	3/4 cup
1/3 cup	**Cherry Yogurt** *low fat*	1/2 cup
2 Tbsp.	**Applesauce** *unsweetened*	1/4 cup
2 tsp.	**Brown Sugar**	1 Tbsp.
1 1/2 tsp.	**Yeast** *fast rise*	2 tsp.
	- or -	
2 tsp.	**Yeast** *active dry*	3 tsp.

This sweet bread, featuring choice dried Bing cherries, is surprisingly versatile. You can use it in lieu of raisin bread for French toast, or serve it warm with cream cheese and honey for a dessert bread. The applesauce and yogurt contribute a refreshing moistness to this light loaf.

Success Hints

- We used Chukar brand cherries, available in our accessory section and gourmet food stores.

- Use low fat fruited yogurt.

- Add the dried cherries whole.

- This recipe can be used with the regular and rapid bake cycles.

regular loaf		large loaf
3/4 cup	**Water**	1 1/8 cup
2 cups	**White Bread Flour**	3 cups
1 Tbsp.	**Dry Milk**	1 1/2 Tbsp.
1 1/2 Tbsp.	**Sugar**	2 Tbsp.
1 tsp.	**Salt**	1 1/2 tsp.
1 Tbsp.	**Butter**	2 Tbsp.
1 tsp.	**Yeast** *fast rise*	2 tsp.
	- or -	
1 1/2 tsp.	**Yeast** *active dry*	3 tsp.

Classic White

Calories 171   Protein 12%
Cholesterol 4.54 mg.   Carbohydrates 77 %
Sodium 323 mg.   Fat 11%

Nutritional information per serving

This is a classic - plain white bread, but a world away from store bought. This loaf's light bodied texture makes it the standard for sandwich breads or the perfect accompaniment for meals. Bake it while you're still deciding what's for dinner; like most classics, its versatility lies in its simplicity.

Success Hints

- Classic White makes great low fat croutons. Lightly butter bread slices, cube, and bake at 350° until crisp.

- Classic White is the perfect bread for sampling the savory and sweet spreads on pages 142 - 143.

- This recipe can be made with the regular, rapid, or delayed time bake cycles.

Raisin Bread

Calories 168   Protein 10 %
Cholesterol 4.54 mg. Carbohydrates 79 %
Sodium 248 mg.   Fat 11 %

Nutritional information per serving

regular loaf		large loaf
3/4 cup	**Water**	1 1/4 cups
2 cups	**White Bread Flour**	3 cups
1 Tbsp.	**Dry Milk**	2 Tbsp.
1 Tbsp.	**Sugar**	1 1/2 Tbsp.
1 tsp.	**Salt**	1 1/2 tsp.
1 Tbsp.	**Butter**	2 Tbsp.
1/2 tsp.	**Cinnamon**	1 tsp.
1/2 cup	**Raisins**	1 cup
1 1/2 tsp.	**Yeast** *fast rise*	2 tsp.
	- or -	
2 tsp.	**Yeast** *active dry*	3 tsp.

Raisin bread is one of life's simple pleasures - and just about everyone's all-time favorite breakfast bread. Our recipe blends the fruit right into the loaf unless you add the raisins in mid-cycle; it's your choice. Either way, this promises to be one of your best breads for French toast.

Success Hints

- For whole raisins in the bread, add fruit at the beep on the fruit and nut cycle or after the first knead.

- If using rapid bake cycle, add raisins with other ingredients.

- For a real taste delight, try with Honey Butter spread - page 143.

- This recipe can be made with the regular, rapid, or delayed time bake cycles.

100% Whole Wheat

Calories 125   Protein 14 %
Cholesterol 3.98 mg.   Carbohydrates 73 %
Sodium 218 mg.   Fat 13 %

Nutritional information per serving

regular loaf		large loaf
1 cup	**Water**	1 1/2 cups + 2 Tbsp.
2 1/2 cups	**Wheat Bread Flour**	3 3/4 cups
1 1/4 Tbsp.	**Dry Milk**	2 Tbsp.
1 tsp.	**Salt**	1 1/2 tsp.
1 1/2 Tbsp.	**Butter**	2 Tbsp.
1 1/4 Tbsp.	**Honey**	2 Tbsp.
1 Tbsp.	**Gluten**	1 1/2 Tbsp.
2 tsp.	**Molasses**	1 Tbsp.
1 1/2 tsp.	**Yeast** *fast rise*	2 1/8 tsp.
	- or -	
2 tsp.	**Yeast** *active dry*	3 tsp.

The trick to making 100% whole wheat bread in your machine is an extra knead, which gives the yeast and gluten a second chance to create a lighter loaf. When your first knead cycle is completed, simply reset the machine and start again. Some manufacturers produce home bakeries with a whole wheat cycle; if your machine doesn't have one, our start-again method works as an easy alternative.

Success Hints

■ The gluten gives the whole wheat flour the structure necessary for a good loaf. If your market doesn't stock wheat gluten, try your local health food store.

■ Remember the extra knead. It's especially important in 100% whole wheat bread.

■ Because of the extra knead, we use this recipe only on the regular bake cycle.

Swedish Limpa

Calories 158   Protein 12 %
Cholesterol 5.30 mg. Carbohydrates 74 %
Sodium 288 mg.   Fat 14 %

Nutritional information per serving

This rich but light rye is the corner-stone of a traditional Swedish break-fast. The anise and orange peel add just a kiss of flavor to complement the rye. Our Swedish friend, Carina Saunders, says to serve limpa with a slice of cheese, a soft-boiled egg in an egg cup, and a cup of strong black coffee. *Ja!*

Success Hints

- We produced our flat ale by opening a dark beer and stirring until the bubbles were dispersed. Scoop off residual foam before measuring ale.

- This recipe can be made with the regular and rapid bake cycles.

regular loaf		large loaf
1/4 cup	**Water**	1/2 cup
1 3/4 cups	**White Bread Flour**	2 1/2 cups
1/4 cup	**Rye Flour**	1/2 cup
1 Tbsp.	**Dry Milk**	2 Tbsp.
1 tsp.	**Salt**	1 1/2 tsp.
1 Tbsp.	**Butter**	2 Tbsp.
3/4 Tbsp.	**Honey**	1 Tbsp.
3/4 Tbsp.	**Molasses**	1 Tbsp.
1/2 cup	**Flat Ale**	3/4 cup
1/4 tsp.	**Cardamom**	1/2 tsp.
1/4 tsp.	**Anise Seed**	1/2 tsp.
1/2 Tbsp.	**Orange Peel**	1 Tbsp.
1 tsp.	**Yeast** fast rise	2 tsp.
	- or -	
2 tsp.	**Yeast** active dry	3 tsp.

Tropical Medley

Calories 178   Protein 10 %
Cholesterol 5.3 mg.   Carbohydrates 77 %
Sodium 289 mg.   Fat 13 %

Nutritional information per serving

regular loaf		large loaf
3/4 cup	**Water**	1 1/4 cup
2 cups	**White Bread Flour**	3 cups
1 Tbsp.	**Dry Milk**	2 Tbsp.
1 Tbsp.	**Sugar**	1 1/2 Tbsp.
1 tsp.	**Salt**	1 1/2 tsp.
1 Tbsp.	**Butter**	2 Tbsp.
1/2 cup	**Dried Fruit Mix**	1 cup
1 1/2 tsp.	**Yeast** *fast rise*	2 tsp.
	- or -	
2 1/4 tsp.	**Yeast** *active dry*	3 tsp.

This is a light, colorful bread full of fruity surprises. Because of the variety in the dried fruit mix, each bite has a different flavor. Moms love this bread for its wholesomeness and kids love it for its natural sweetness.

Success Hints

- Apricots, coconut, golden raisins, papaya and pineapple make a good combination for the dried fruit mix.

- Several brands of pre-chopped and pre-packaged "Tropical Medley" mix are available - great for fast preparation.

- You don't need to use the fruit and nut cycle; simply add the dried fruit with your other ingredients.

- This recipe can be made with the regular, rapid or delayed time bake cycles.

Kulich

Calories 200   Protein 13 %
Cholesterol 36.0 mg. Carbohydrates 76 %
Sodium 238 mg.   Fat 11 %

Nutritional information per serving

		regular loaf	large loaf
1/2 cup	**Water**		3/4 cup
2 cups + 2 Tbsp.	**White Bread Flour**		3 1/4 cups
1 tsp.	**Salt**		1 1/2 tsp.
1	**Eggs**		2
2 Tbsp.	**Raisins**		1/4 cup
2 Tbsp.	**Dried Cherries**		1/4 cup
2 Tbsp.	**Dried Fruit Mix**		1/4 cup
2 Tbsp.	**Milk**		1/4 cup
2 Tbsp.	**Honey**		3 Tbsp.
3/4 tsp.	**Vanilla Extract**		1 tsp.
1/4 tsp.	**Lemon Peel** *dried*		1/2 tsp.
2 Tbsp.	**Toasted Almonds**		1/4 cup
1 tsp.	**Yeast** *fast rise*		1 1/2 tsp.
	- or -		
2 tsp.	**Yeast** *active dry*		3 tsp.

Sasha, our photographer, says that in the Soviet Union, this traditional Russian Easter bread is baked in small loaves and given for good luck to friends who come to visit. Your visitors will think they're lucky, too, if you serve this festive loaf. Topped with the traditional sweet Paskha, it's one of our brunch favorites *any* day of the year.

Success Hints

- Brush bread with a mixture of 1 Tbsp. honey, 1 Tbsp. lemon juice and 1 Tbsp. triple sec while still hot for a glazed finish.

- Paskha transforms this from a wonderful sweet fruit loaf to a spectacular dessert bread. Our recipe for this traditional topping is on page 143.

- If dried cherries are unavailable where you live, double the dried mixed fruit. Dried cherries are available in our accessories section.

- Toast almonds lightly by browning in a 350° oven for five minutes, stirring frequently.

- This recipe can be baked using the regular and rapid bake cycles.

Multi-Grain and More

Calories 137   Protein 12 %
Cholesterol 4.54 mg. Carbohydrates 74 %
Sodium 249 mg.   Fat 16 %

Nutritional information per serving

We call this bread "Multi-Grain and More" because it's so packed with good-for-you stuff. All those grains give it a full, rich flavor - and enough body to stick to your ribs. If you want the benefits of cereal and the timeliness of toast, this is the bread for you.

Success Hints

- Any unsweetened multi-grain cereal should work in this bread.

- For accent and crunch, sprinkle a few oats on top after the final rise, just before baking.

- Try with Gruyere Apple Spread - page 143.

- This recipe can be made with the regular, rapid, or delayed time bake cycles.

regular loaf		large loaf
3/4 cup	**Water**	1 1/4 cups
1 1/4 cups	**White Bread Flour**	2 1/4 cups
1/4 cup	**Wheat Bread Flour**	1/2 cup
1 Tbsp.	**Dry Milk**	2 Tbsp.
1 tsp.	**Salt**	1 1/2 tsp.
1 Tbsp.	**Butter**	2 Tbsp.
1/4 cup	**7 Grain Rolled Cereal**	1/2 cup
2 Tbsp.	**Wheat Germ**	3 Tbsp.
1 Tbsp.	**Oat Bran**	2 Tbsp.
1 Tbsp.	**Cracked Wheat**	2 Tbsp.
1 1/2 Tbsp.	**Honey**	2 1/2 Tbsp.
1 tsp.	**Yeast** fast rise	2 tsp.
	- or -	
1 1/2 tsp.	**Yeast** active dry	3 tsp.

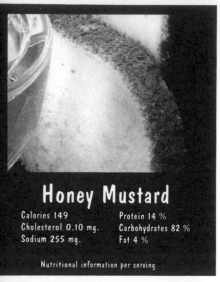

Honey Mustard

Calories 149
Cholesterol 0.10 mg.
Sodium 255 mg.

Protein 14 %
Carbohydrates 82 %
Fat 4 %

Nutritional information per serving

You don't need to love mustard to love this bread. The mustard adds a subtle, secondary flavor. This bread makes an unforgettable ham sandwich, or it can be served warm with baked ham or roast duck.

regular loaf		large loaf
1/2 cup	**Water**	3/4 cup
1 1/2 cups	**White Bread Flour**	2 cups
1/2 cup	**Wheat Bread Flour**	1 cup
2 tsp.	**Dry Milk**	1 Tbsp.
2 1/2 Tbsp.	**Honey**	1/4 cup
1/2 tsp.	**Salt**	1 tsp.
1/4 cup	**Chicken Broth** *low salt/canned*	1/2 cup
1 2/3 Tbsp.	**Gourmet Mustard**	2 1/2 Tbsp.
1 tsp.	**Chives** *dried*	2 tsp.
1 tsp.	**Yeast** *fast rise*	2 tsp.
2 tsp.	*- or -* **Yeast** *active dry*	3 tsp.

Success Hints

■ We like Grey Poupon Country Dijon Mustard in this recipe.

■ Experiment with your favorite mustard flavors.

■ This recipe can be made with the regular and rapid bake cycles.

Apple Oat

Calories 157　　　Protein 12 %
Cholesterol 2.72 mg.　　Carbohydrates 79 %
Sodium 262 mg.　　Fat 9 %

Nutritional information per serving

This is a full-bodied oatmeal bread with the added sweetness of apples and honey. It goes well with smoked meats such as summer sausage. For something different, try a curried turkey salad filling.

Success Hints

- Use unsweetened apples, canned in water. Drain well and chop into chunks.

- Use frozen apple juice concentrate, thawed, with no water added.

- This recipe can be made with the regular or rapid bake cycles.

regular loaf		large loaf
1/2 cup	**Water**	3/4 cups
1 1/3 cups	**White Bread Flour**	2 cups
2/3 cup	**Wheat Bread Flour**	1 cup
2 tsp.	**Dry Milk**	1 Tbsp.
1 tsp.	**Salt**	1 1/2 tsp.
2 tsp.	**Butter**	1 Tbsp.
1/2 cup	**Apples** canned/chopped	3/4 cup
1 Tbsp.	**Apple Juice** concentrated	2 Tbsp.
2 tsp.	**Lemon Juice**	1 Tbsp.
1 Tbsp.	**Honey**	2 Tbsp.
2 Tbsp.	**Yogurt**	1/4 cup
2 tsp.	**Molasses**	1 Tbsp.
1/4 cup	**Oats**	1/2 cup
1 tsp.	**Yeast** fast rise	1 1/2 tsp.
	- or -	
2 tsp.	**Yeast** active dry	3 tsp.

Peanut Butter

Calories 207   Protein 13 %
Cholesterol 0 mg.   Carbohydrates 62 %
Sodium 143 mg.   Fat 25 %

Nutritional information per serving

		regular loaf	large loaf
3/4 cup	**Water**	1 1/4 cups
2 cups	**White Bread Flour**	3 cups
2 1/2 Tbsp.	**Brown Sugar**	1/4 cup
1/4 tsp.	**Salt**	1/2 tsp.
1/3 cup.	**Peanut Butter**	1/2 cup
1 tsp.	**Yeast** *fast rise*	2 tsp.
- or -		
2 tsp.	**Yeast** *active dry*	3 tsp.

Jim, our unofficial humorist, says, "At last, a peanut butter that doesn't stick to the roof of your mouth!" Top with honey or jam for a peanut butter sandwich in half the time. Although kids devour it, don't forget to share the fun and flavor with a few grown ups, too.

Success Hints

- Use your choice of creamy or crunchy quality peanut butter.

- Fill with jam and cut into fun shapes for a pre-school luncheon or children's party.

- This recipe can be made with the regular, rapid, or delayed time bake cycles.

Certainly Citrus

Calories 175   Protein 11 %
Cholesterol 5.53 mg. Carbohydrates 76 %
Sodium 302 mg.   Fat 13 %

Nutritional information per serving

This tangy bread has a fine, light texture. The subtle yet distinctive flavor makes it a perfect accompaniment for fish or chicken. Try it with swordfish baked with lime butter or your favorite lemon chicken recipe.

Success Hints

- If using fresh lemon peel, zest very fine and avoid using the white pulp.

- The crust on this bread is a naturally light color.

- Try this bread with the Cheesy Lemon spread - page 143.

- This recipe can be made with the regular and rapid bake cycles.

regular loaf		large loaf
2/3 cup	**Water**	1 cup
2 cups	**White Bread Flour**	3 cups
1 Tbsp. + 1 tsp.	**Dry Milk**	2 Tbsp.
2 tsp.	**Sugar**	1 Tbsp.
1 tsp.	**Salt**	1 1/2 tsp.
1 Tbsp. + 1 tsp.	**Butter**	2 Tbsp.
2 Tbsp.	**Orange Marmalade**	1/4 cup
2 tsp.	**Lemon Juice**	1 Tbsp.
2 tsp.	**Lime Juice**	1 Tbsp.
pinch	**Lemon Peel**	1/8 tsp.
1 tsp.	**Yeast** fast rise	1 1/2 tsp.
	- or -	
2 tsp.	**Yeast** active dry	3 tsp.

Cottage Dill

Calories 151
Cholesterol 1.28 mg.
Sodium 329 mg.

Protein 18 %
Carbohydrates 78 %
Fat 4 %

Nutritional information per serving

regular loaf		large loaf
1/2 cup	**Water**	3/4 cups
2 cups	**White Bread Flour**	3 cups
1 Tbsp.	**Dry Milk**	1 1/2 Tbsp.
1 Tbsp.	**Sugar**	2 Tbsp.
1 tsp.	**Salt**	1 1/2 tsp.
1 Tbsp.	**Butter**	1 1/2 Tbsp.
1/4 cup	**Cottage Cheese**	3/4 cup
1/2 Tbsp.	**Dry Onion**	1 Tbsp.
1/2 Tbsp.	**Dill Seed**	1 Tbsp.
1/2 Tbsp.	**Dill Weed**	1 Tbsp.
1 tsp.	**Yeast** *fast rise*	2 tsp.
	- or -	
2 tsp.	**Yeast** *active dry*	3 tsp.

This bread will make a bread machine believer out of anyone. The aroma is heaven, and the taste lives up to the aroma. Cottage Dill is best served warm from the oven or toaster; the heat liberates the spices for a full, rich flavor.

Success Hints

- Use small curd, low fat cottage cheese.

- The liquid in cottage cheese varies. If your dough is too dry, try adding water a tablespoon at a time during the kneading until dough appears moist and pliable.

- This recipe can be made with the regular or rapid bake cycles.

Cajun Spice

Calories 154   Protein 12 %
Cholesterol 5.30 mg.   Carbohydrates 74 %
Sodium 468 mg.   Fat 14 %

Nutritional information per serving

This is not a shy little bread to quench the fire of jambalaya or your blackened redfish. This is a bread with legs, bread that will get up and dance to Zydeco music all by itself! The Cajun spice mix promises to send a wake-up call to your taste buds when you serve it with salad or red beans and rice.

Success Hints

- Paul Prudhomme's Seafood Magic Spice is a great Cajun blend to use.

- Morton and Bassett makes a tasty salt-free Cajun blend. If using a no-salt blend, double the amount of the spice mix in the recipe.

- If using other spice blends, you may need to adjust the spice and salt amounts.

regular loaf		large loaf
3/4 cup	Water	1 1/8 cups
2 cups	White Bread Flour	3 cups
1 Tbsp.	Dry Milk	2 Tbsp.
1/2 tsp.	Salt	1 tsp.
1 Tbsp.	Butter	2 Tbsp.
1 Tbsp.	Brown Sugar	1 1/2 Tbsp.
1 Tbsp.	Cajun Spice Blend	1 1/2 Tbsp.
2 tsp.	Tomato Paste	1 Tbsp.
1/2 tsp.	Onion Paste	1 tsp.
1/4 tsp.	Parsley Flakes	1/2 tsp.
1 1/4 tsp.	Yeast *fast rise*	2 tsp.
	- or -	
2 tsp.	Yeast *active dry*	3 tsp.

- Onion powder may be substituted for onion paste, 1/4 teaspoon for a large loaf, and 1/8 teaspoon for a regular.

- This recipe can be made with the regular or rapid bake cycles.

Almond Poppy

Calories 179   Protein 12 %
Cholesterol 4.09 mg. Carbohydrates 65 %
Sodium 180 mg.   Fat 23 %

Nutritional information per serving

		regular loaf		large loaf
	1/2 cup	**Water**	3/4 cup
	2 cups	**White Bread Flour**	3 cups
	1 Tbsp.	**Dry Milk**	1 1/2 Tbsp.
	1/2 tsp.	**Salt**	1 tsp.
	1 Tbsp.	**Butter**	1 1/2 Tbsp.
	1/4 cup	**Lemon Yogurt**	3/4 cup
	1 1/2 Tbsp.	**Honey**	2 Tbsp.
	1/4 cup	**Almonds** *sliced & toasted*	1/2 Cup
	2 tsp.	**Lemon Peel** *dried*	1 Tbsp.
	2 Tbsp.	**Poppy Seeds**	3 Tbsp.
	1 tsp.	**Lemon Extract**	2 tsp.
	1 tsp.	**Yeast** *fast rise*	2 tsp.
		- or -	
	2 tsp.	**Yeast** *active dry*	3 tsp.

This soft yellow bread is reminiscent of your favorite poppy seed muffin, but versatile enough to take you from breakfast to dessert. Start the day enjoying it with a touch of sweet butter on a freshly toasted slice. Savor with tea in the afternoon. After dinner, celebrate this winning dessert bread by topping slices with our Cheesy Lemon spread. Mmmmm.

Success Hints

- Toast almonds lightly in a shallow pan. *Stirring frequently,* bake at 350° for five minutes or until golden brown.

- For a luscious dessert bread, serve with the Cheesy Lemon spread - page 143.

- This recipe can be made with the regular and rapid bake cycles.

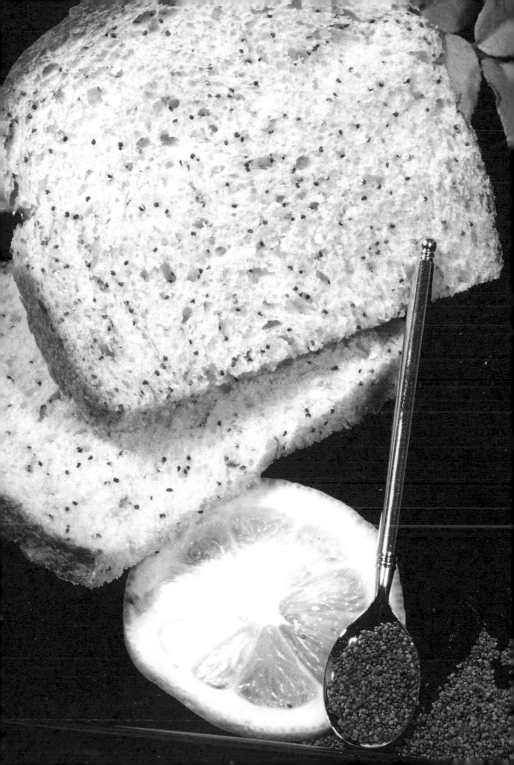

Honey Wheat

Calories 148   Protein 12 %
Cholesterol 5.27 mg.   Carbohydrates 74 %
Sodium 287 mg.   Fat 14 %
Nutritional information per serving

regular loaf		large loaf
3/4 cup	**Water**	1 1/8 cups
1 1/2 cups	**White Bread Flour**	2 1/2 cups
1/2 cup	**Wheat Bread Flour**	1/2 cup
1 Tbsp.	**Dry Milk**	1 1/2 Tbsp.
1 Tbsp.	**Honey**	1 1/2 Tbsp.
1 tsp.	**Salt**	1 1/2 tsp.
1 Tbsp.	**Butter**	2 Tbsp.
1 tsp.	**Yeast** *fast rise*	2 tsp.
	- or -	
1 1/2 tsp.	**Yeast** *active dry*	3 tsp.

Want to know how far you can go with this bread? Our friend, Ed Rasmuson, even takes his bread machine hunting! The first year Ed took his home bakery on his annual trek to Kodiak, he caught some razzing. But eight days and eight loaves later, his buddies were hooked. "They all kind of laughed when I bought my bread machine," Ed reports, "but they don't laugh anymore." A basic whole wheat like this is one of the group's favorites.

Success Hints

- Just follow the recipe, use a good bread flour, and you can't go wrong.

- Try this bread with our Honey Butter - page 143.

- This recipe can be made with the regular, rapid, or delayed time bake cycles.

Garlic

Calories 203   Protein 22 %
Cholesterol 15.1 mg.   Carbohydrates 50 %
Sodium 443 mg.   Fat 28 %

Nutritional information per serving

regular loaf		large loaf
3/4 cup	**Water**	1 cup + 2 Tbsp.
2 cups + 1 Tbsp.	**White Bread Flour**	3 cups + 2 Tbsp.
1 Tbsp.	**Sugar**	1 1/2 Tbsp.
1/2 tsp.	**Salt**	3/4 tsp.
1/2 Tbsp.	**Butter**	3/4 Tbsp.
2 Tbsp.	**Parmesan** *fresh/grated*	3 Tbsp.
1/2 tsp.	**Sweet Basil**	3/4 tsp.
1/2 tsp.	**Garlic Powder**	3/4 tsp.
1/2 tsp.	**Garlic Paste**	3/4 tsp.
3/4 tsp.	**Yeast** *fast rise*	1 tsp.
	- or -	
1 1/2 tsp.	**Yeast** *active dry*	2 tsp.

When Lynn put her house on the market, we offered this advice: "If you want to sell your house, bake garlic bread when people are coming through!" The aroma of this bread is to die for - and it butters up to make the easiest garlic toast around.

Success Hints

- Grate your own fresh parmesan cheese. Pre-ground cheeses often have salt in them.

- Serve this bread warm. The flavor is definitely enhanced.

- Finely chopped or pressed garlic may be substituted for paste. Use 1/4 tsp. for a regular loaf, 1/2 tsp. for large.

- This recipe can be made with the regular and rapid bake cycles.

Saffron

Calories 164   Protein 13 %
Cholesterol 18.6 mg. Carbohydrates 69 %
Sodium 288 mg.   Fat 18 %

Nutritional information per serving

regular loaf		large loaf
3/4 cup	**Water**	1 1/4 cup
2 cups	**White Bread Flour**	3 cups
1 tsp.	**Sugar**	1/2 Tbsp.
1 tsp.	**Salt**	1 1/2 tsp.
1	**Egg** *beaten*	1
1 1/2 Tbsp.	**Olive Oil**	2 Tbsp.
1/4 tsp.	**Saffron** *ground*	1/2 tsp.
	- or -	
1/8 tsp.	**Saffron** *threads*	1/4 tsp.
1 tsp.	**Yeast** *fast rise*	2 tsp.
	- or -	
2 tsp.	**Yeast** *active dry*	3 tsp.

Saffron is the world's most expensive spice - 225,000 crocus stigmas are needed to make a single pound! The texture and flavor of this light and fluffy loaf will convince you it's worth it. This is bread for a special occasion - or bread that will make any occasion special. The distinctive Old World flavor works magic with seafood and hearty soups like lentil or sausage.

Success Hints

■ If using Saffron thread, grind to a coarse powder-like consistency using a mortar and pestle. The fresh powder will be more potent than the pre-ground, so you'll need less.

■ Once opened, the intensity of a vial of saffron will diminish.

■ This recipe can be made with the regular or rapid bake cycles.

Maraschino Pecan

Calories 162   Protein 11 %
Cholesterol 2.3 mg.   Carbohydrates 68 %
Sodium 201 mg.   Fat 21 %

Nutritional information per serving

regular loaf		large loaf
3/4 cup	**Water**	1 1/8 cups
2 cups	**White Bread Flour**	3 cups
1 Tbsp.	**Dry Milk**	1 1/2 Tbsp.
1 Tbsp. & 1 tsp.	**Sugar**	2 Tbsp.
3/4 tsp.	**Salt**	1 1/4 tsp.
2 tsp.	**Butter**	1 Tbsp.
2 1/2 Tbsp.	**Raisins**	1/4 cup
2 1/2 Tbsp.	**Maraschino Cherries**	1/4 cup
2 1/2 Tbsp.	**Sunflower Seeds**	1/4 cup
2 1/2 Tbsp.	**Pecans** chopped	1/4 cup
Pinch	**Ground Cinnamon**	1/8 tsp.
Pinch	**Ground Ginger**	1/8 tsp.
1 1/2 tsp.	**Yeast** fast rise	2 tsp.
	- or -	
2 tsp.	**Yeast** active dry	3 tsp.

You can dress this bread up or down, and you'll love it either way. Combine green and red maraschino cherries for a festive holiday bread, or substitute your favorite dried fruits for a sweet morning meal with a light crunch. The pecans offer a perfect counterpart to the fruit.

Success Hints

- Drain cherries well on a paper towel.

- Add cherries whole for appearance.

- Add the fruit and nuts at the beep on the fruit and nut cycle or at the end of the first knead.

- Replace half the cherries with chopped dried apricots, pears, dates or apples.

- This recipe can be made with the regular, rapid, or delayed time bake cycles.

Easy French

Calories 132
Cholesterol 0 mg.
Sodium 247 mg.
Protein 13 %
Carbohydrates 84 %
Fat 3 %

Nutritional information per serving

regular loaf		large loaf
3/4 cup + 1 Tbsp.	**Water**	1 1/2 cups
2 cups	**White Bread Flour**	3 1/4 cups
1 Tbsp.	**Sugar**	1 1/2 Tbsp.
1 tsp.	**Salt**	1 1/2 tsp.
1 tsp.	**Yeast** *fast rise*	2 tsp.
	- or -	
1 1/2 tsp.	**Yeast** *active dry*	3 tsp.

Our Easy French is exactly that - *easy*. It may look a little different, but from its crusty crust to its light, chewy interior, it tastes great. This recipe was created for machines without a French bread baking cycle: it mixes, rises and bakes entirely in your machine. Or you can make a traditional loaf from this recipe using our Picnic Basket process instructions on page 138.

Success Hints

■ To develop the crisp crust that French bread is known for, turn the machine off and reset it after the first knead cycle is completed. This gives the bread extra kneading time and results in a crisp crust.

■ When the bread comes out of the machine, the crust color may look light to you. This is normal for this loaf.

■ This recipe can be used with regular and rapid bake cycles.

62

Light Rye

Calories 158
Cholesterol 3.53 mg.
Sodium 255 mg.

Protein 12 %
Carbohydrates 77 %
Fat 11 %

Nutritional information per serving

In the mood for your favorite ham and cheese sandwich? This is the bread for you. This light loaf was created with sandwiches in mind. Slice it, fill it, and let your tastebuds take it from there.

Success Hints

- Just follow the recipe. It's that easy!

- This recipe can be made with the regular, rapid, or delayed time bake cycles.

regular loaf		large loaf
3/4 cup	**Water**	1 cup + 2 Tbsp.
1 1/2 cups	**White Bread Flour**	2 1/4 cups
1/2 cup	**Rye Flour**	3/4 cup
1 1/2 Tbsp.	**Sugar**	2 1/2 Tbsp.
3/4 tsp.	**Salt**	1 1/4 tsp.
3/4 Tbsp.	**Butter**	1 1/4 Tbsp.
2 tsp.	**Cornmeal**	1 Tbsp.
1 tsp.	**Caraway Seeds**	1/2 Tbsp.
1 1/4 tsp.	**Yeast** *fast rise*	2 tsp.
	- or -	
2 tsp.	**Yeast** *active dry*	3 tsp.

Sweet Coconut Curry

Calories 176   Protein 10 %
Cholesterol 4.89 mg. Carbohydrates 74 %
Sodium 274 mg.   Fat 16 %

Nutritional information per serving

Colorful and unexpected, this bread is as distinctive as the country that inspired it. The raisins and coconut lend a slight sweetness, but the flavor and aroma are distinctly curry. Serve it with your favorite rice and meat dish.

Success Hints

- If you like more kick in your curry, use hot curry.

- This recipe can be made with the regular, rapid, or delayed time bake cycles.

regular loaf		large loaf
3/4 cup	Water	1 1/4 cup
2 cups	White Bread Flour	3 cups
1 Tbsp.	Dry Milk	2 Tbsp.
1 Tbsp.	Brown Sugar	2 Tbsp.
1 tsp.	Salt	1 1/2 tsp.
1 Tbsp.	Butter	2 Tbsp.
1/3 cup	Raisins	1/2 cup
1/3 cup	Coconut Flakes	1/2 cup
2 tsp.	Curry Powder	1 Tbsp.
1 1/2 tsp.	Yeast *fast rise*	2 tsp.
	- or -	
2 tsp.	Yeast *active dry*	3 tsp.

Carrot

Calories 143   Protein 13 %
Cholesterol 0.33 mg. Carbohydrates 84 %
Sodium 258 mg.   Fat 3 %

Nutritional information per serving

Getting your beta carotene was never this easy - or this tasty. The wheat flour gives this bread body, the nuts and carrots give it texture, and the yogurt keeps it moist. Serve this bread with steaming bowls of vegetable soup for a nutritious, hearty lunch.

Success Hints

- Use freshly grated carrots.

- This recipe can be made with the regular and rapid bake cycles.

regular loaf		large loaf
1/2 cup	**Water**	3/4 cups
1 1/3 cups	**White Bread Flour**	2 1/4 cups
2/3 cup	**Wheat Bread Flour**	1 cup
2 tsp.	**Dry Milk**	1 Tbsp.
1 tsp.	**Salt**	1 1/2 tsp.
2/3 cup	**Carrots** grated	1 cup
1 Tbsp.	**Honey**	2 Tbsp.
2 Tbsp.	**Yogurt** plain	1/4 cup
1 Tbsp.	**Molasses**	2 Tbsp.
2 Tbsp.	**Walnuts** chopped	1/4 cup
1 tsp.	**Yeast** fast rise	1 1/2 tsp.
	- or -	
2 tsp.	**Yeast** active dry	2 1/2 tsp.

Italian Wheat

Calories 183 Protein 11 %
Cholesterol 0.65 mg. Carbohydrates 57 %
Sodium 150 mg. Fat 32 %

Nutritional information per serving

regular loaf		large loaf
1/2 cup + 2 Tbsp.	**Water**	1 cup
1 1/2 cups	**White Bread Flour**	2 cups
1/2 cup	**Wheat Bread Flour**	1 cup
1 Tbsp.	**Sugar**	1 1/2 Tbsp.
1/2 tsp.	**Salt**	3/4 tsp.
1/4 cup	**Pesto Sauce**	1/3 cup
1 tsp.	**Yeast** *fast rise*	2 tsp.
- or -		
1 1/2 tsp.	**Yeast** *active dry*	3 tsp.

The combination of easy preparation and fabulous flavor create a
bread that makes a terrific impres-
sion without much work. This is a
light wheat bread with a succulent
pesto flavor. Serve it plain or use it
for garlic bread with spaghetti or
lasagna.

Success Hints

- Use a freshly prepared pesto sauce
  or make your own. Stir the sauce
  well before measuring to blend oil.

- Make a quick slice of pizza by topping with marinara sauce and cheese,
  then toast under the broiler.

- This recipe can be made with the
  regular and rapid bake cycles.

Bits o' Bacon

Calories 164   Protein 12 %
Cholesterol 6.95 mg. Carbohydrates 69 %
Sodium 317 mg.   Fat 19 %

Nutritional information per serving

The preparations for this bread may be a little more complex than most, but don't be put off - the finished product is definitely worth it. This is one of those loaves the whole family eats up, right out of the oven. If it lasts long enough, this tasty loaf enlivens any soup or salad.

Success Hints

■ Cook bacon until almost crisp. Set bacon fat aside while you crumble cooked bacon, then remix bacon and fat before measuring.

■ Extra pepper may be added to taste.

■ After loaf is partially cooled, brush with butter and sprinkle a little coarsely ground salt on top.

■ This recipe can be made with the regular and rapid bake cycles.

regular loaf		large loaf
2/3 cup	**Water**	1 cup
1 2/3 cups	**White Bread Flour**	2 1/2 cups
1/3 cup	**Wheat Bread Flour**	1/2 cup
4 tsp.	**Sugar**	2 Tbsp.
1 tsp.	**Salt**	1 1/2 tsp.
4 tsp.	**Butter**	2 Tbsp.
1/2 tsp.	**Green Pepper Corns** dried/crushed	3/4 tsp.
1/2 tsp.	**Sweet Basil** dried	3/4 tsp.
pinch	**Garlic Powder**	1/4 tsp.
1/4 cup	**Bacon** with fat	1/3 cup
1 tsp.	**Yeast** fast rise	1 1/2 tsp.
	- or -	
2 tsp.	**Yeast** active dry	2 1/2 tsp.

Saucy Apple

Calories 147   Protein 12 %
Cholesterol 18.0 mg.   Carbohydrates 74 %
Sodium 276 mg.   Fat 14 %

Nutritional information per serving

Did you ever hear the cooking tip about putting a slice of fresh apple in your cake saver to keep your cake moist? Well, the fresh Granny Smith apple in this recipe works the same way in this tangy, long-lasting bread. Even days later, it retains a nice moistness that makes it a favorite for those times when you need to bake ahead.

Success Hints

- Core and dice unpeeled apple.

- The Granny Smith apple adds a tartness to the bread. For a sweeter bread, try using a Rome or a McIntosh.

- This recipe can be made with the regular and rapid bake cycles.

regular loaf		large loaf
1/2 cup	**Apple Cider**	3/4 cup
1 1/3 cups	**White Bread Flour**	2 cups
3/4 cup + 1 Tbsp.	**Wheat Bread Flour**	1 1/4 cups
1 tsp.	**Salt**	1 1/2 tsp.
2 1/2 Tbsp.	**Yogurt** plain	1/4 cup
2 1/2 Tbsp.	**Honey**	1/4 cup
1/3 tsp.	**Vanilla**	1/2 tsp.
2 1/2 Tbsp.	**Walnuts** unchopped	1/4 cup
2 1/2 Tbsp.	**Egg** beaten	1
1/3 cup	**Applesauce** unsweetened	1/2 cup
1/3 cup	**Granny Smith Apple** unpeeled	1/2 cup
3/4 tsp.	**Yeast** fast rise	1 1/4 tsp.
	- or -	
1 1/4 tsp.	**Yeast** active dry	2 tsp.

Baked Potato

Calories 160   Protein 13 %
Cholesterol 4.79 mg. Carbohydrates 72 %
Sodium 285 mg.   Fat 15 %

Nutritional information per serving

regular loaf		large loaf
1/2 cup	**Water**	3/4 cup
2 cups	**White Bread Flour**	3 cups
1 Tbsp.	**Dry Milk**	1 1/2 Tbsp.
1 Tbsp.	**Sugar**	1 1/2 Tbsp.
1 tsp.	**Salt**	1 1/2 tsp.
1/4 cup	**Sour Cream**	1/2 cup
1 1/2 Tbsp.	**Potato Flakes** *instant*	2 1/2 Tbsp.
1 1/2 Tbsp.	**Bacon Bits**	3 Tbsp.
1 1/2 Tbsp.	**Chives**	3 Tbsp.
1 tsp.	**Yeast** *fast rise*	2 tsp.
	- or -	
2 tsp.	**Yeast** *active dry*	3 tsp.

If you are a meat and potatoes kind of person, this is the bread for you. Just add butter, and you have a potato loaf with all the trimmings! The velvety texture and rich flavor make this bread a wonderful companion to roasts, and a natural for meatloaf sandwiches. Served warm, it turns a bowl of vegetable beef soup into a memorable meal.

Success Hints

■ This dough will be very dry. Resist the urge to add water.

■ For best flavor, use real bacon bits.

■ For a taste treat, top with our Jezebel Jam - page 142.

■ This recipe can be baked with the regular or rapid bake cycles.

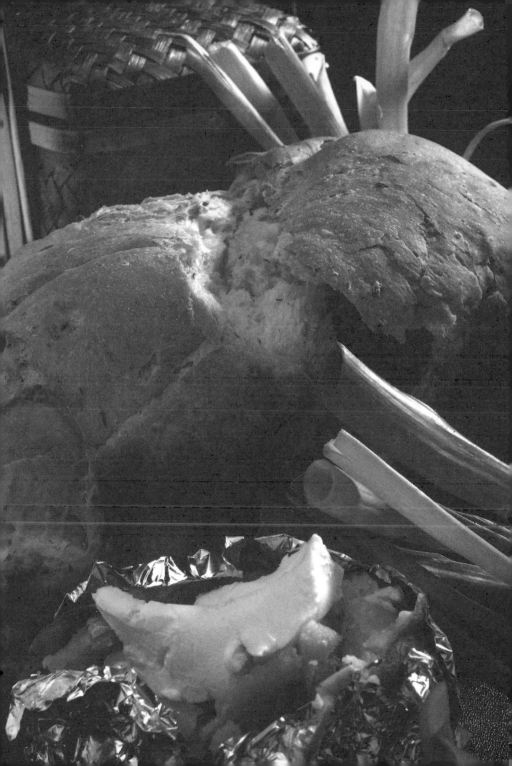

100% Crunch

Calories 147   Protein 13 %
Cholesterol 0 mg.   Carbohydrates 68 %
Sodium 268 mg.   Fat 19 %

Nutritional information per serving

regular loaf		large loaf
3/4 cup + 1 Tbsp.	**Water**	1 1/4 cup + 1 Tbsp.
2 cups	**Wheat Bread Flour**	3 cups
1 tsp.	**Salt**	1 1/2 tsp.
4 tsp.	**Honey**	2 Tbsp.
4 tsp.	**Molasses**	2 Tbsp.
2 tsp.	**Gluten**	1 Tbsp.
4 tsp.	**Olive Oil**	2 Tbsp.
1/2 cup	**Seeds**	2/3 cup
1 tsp.	**Yeast** *fast rise*	2 tsp.
	- or -	
2 tsp.	**Yeast** *active dry*	3 tsp.

We created this bread for people who think 100% whole wheat is boring. The seeds inject a crunchy, chewy texture so satisfying, you won't even need a toaster for crispness. High in fiber and high in taste, 100% Crunch brings a new dimension to an avocado and sprout sandwich.

Success Hints

■ We used equal amounts of pumpkin seeds, flax seeds and sunflower seeds.

■ Try using different seeds for different taste and texture. (No bird seed, please!)

■ For best results, use the "extra knead" process and add seeds near the end of the first knead.

■ Gluten is available in health food stores and nutritional departments.

■ This recipe can be made with the regular, rapid, or time bake cycles.

Garden Herb

Calories 162
Cholesterol 5.53 mg.
Sodium 300 mg.

Protein 12 %
Carbohydrates 74 %
Fat 14 %

Nutritional information per serving

regular loaf		large loaf
3/4 cup	**Water**	1 1/4 cups
2 cups	**White Bread Flour**	3 cups
1 Tbsp.	**Dry Milk**	2 Tbsp.
1 Tbsp.	**Sugar**	2 Tbsp.
1 tsp.	**Salt**	1 1/2 tsp.
1 Tbsp.	**Butter**	2 Tbsp.
1 tsp.	**Chives**	1/2 Tbsp.
1 tsp.	**Marjoram**	1/2 Tbsp.
1 tsp.	**Thyme**	1/2 Tbsp.
1/2 tsp.	**Basil**	1 tsp.
1 tsp.	**Yeast** *fast rise*	2 tsp.
	- or -	
2 tsp.	**Yeast** *active dry*	3 tsp.

The fragrance of turkey stuffing will fill your home while this flavorful bread is baking, thanks to all those aromatic dried herbs. This loaf is excellent for any cold meat sandwich you can dream up - including turkey and cranberry - and it makes down-right tasty croutons.

Success Hints

- Use dried herbs that are flaked and not ground. If using ground, reduce the amount by half. If using fresh herbs, double the amount.

- Any combination of spices may be substituted, according to your tastes.

- To make low fat oven croutons, see the recipe on page 26 (Classic White).

- This recipe can be made with the regular, rapid, or delayed time bake cycles.

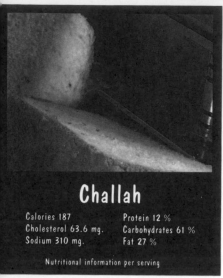

Challah

Calories 187   Protein 12 %
Cholesterol 63.6 mg. Carbohydrates 61 %
Sodium 310 mg.   Fat 27 %

Nutritional information per serving

		regular loaf		large loaf
1/2 cup	**Water**	3/4 cup
2 cups	**White Bread Flour**	3 cups
1 Tbsp.	**Sugar**	2 Tbsp.
1 tsp.	**Salt**	1 1/2 tsp.
2 1/2 Tbsp.	**Butter**	1/4 cup
1	**Eggs**	2
1	**Egg Yolk**	1
1/2 tsp.	**Poppy Seeds**	3/4 tsp.
3/4 tsp.	**Yeast** fast rise	1 1/4 tsp.
	- or -	
1 1/2 tsp.	**Yeast** active dry	2 1/4 tsp.

This light egg bread represents the manna of the desert in Jewish tradition. Like many busy people, Rabbi Harry Rosenfeld of Anchorage's Temple Beth Sholom makes his Sabbath Challah in his home bread machine. "I use it the way it comes out of the machine," he says. "It tastes fine. We use it regularly." For special holidays, the dough can be styled into a variety of shapes.

Success Hints

- For traditional braided Challah, mix ingredients (without poppy seeds) in the dough cycle. Turn dough out onto a floured surface, punch down, divide into ropes and braid, pinching dough together at ends. Top with poppy seeds. Lift onto greased baking sheet and allow to double, about one hour. Bake at 375° for 20-25 minutes. (See recipe for Saffron Braids on page 128 for braiding instructions and illustrations.)

- This egg bread makes great crumbs for Deviled Crab.

- The egg content of this bread makes it a perfect base for a nice rich stuffing.

- This recipe may be baked on the regular or rapid bake cycles.

Mocha Java

Calories 168   Protein 11 %
Cholesterol 21.3 mg.   Carbohydrates 59 %
Sodium 271 mg.   Fat 30 %

Nutritional information per serving

This is a coffee lover's bread. It goes great with a cup of rich French Roast any time of day, making any coffee break feel like a brunch. Serve it with a light spread of cream cheese for an even richer flavor.

Success Hints

- Try your favorite instant coffee mixes, such as Cappuccino or Vienna. Use sugar-free mixes.

- For an alternative, use sugar-free cocoa mix instead of the coffee mix.

- This recipe can be made with regular and rapid bake cycles.

regular loaf		large loaf
3/4 cup	**Water**	1 cup + 2 Tbsp.
1 3/4 cups	**White Bread Flour**	2 1/3 cups
1 Tbsp.	**Dry Milk**	2 Tbsp.
1 tsp.	**Salt**	1 1/2 tsp.
1 1/2 Tbsp.	**Butter**	2 Tbsp.
1/4 cup	**Rye Flour**	1/2 cup
1 1/2 Tbsp.	**Brown Sugar**	2 Tbsp.
1	**Egg**	1
1 Tbsp.	**Instant Mocha** sugarfree coffee mix	2 Tbsp.
1/4 cup	**Pecans** chopped	1/2 cup
1 tsp.	**Yeast** fast rise	2 tsp.
	- or -	
2 tsp.	**Yeast** active dry	3 tsp.

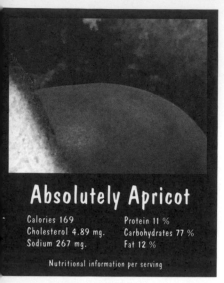

Absolutely Apricot

Calories 169   Protein 11 %
Cholesterol 4.89 mg. Carbohydrates 77 %
Sodium 267 mg.   Fat 12 %

Nutritional information per serving

	regular loaf		large loaf
3/4 cup	**Water**		1 1/4 cup
2 cups	**White Bread Flour**		3 cups
1 Tbsp.	**Dry Milk**		2 Tbsp.
1 tsp.	**Salt**		1 1/2 tsp.
1 Tbsp.	**Butter**		2 Tbsp.
3 Tbsp.	**Apricot Jam**		1/4 cup
1/2 cup	**Dried Apricots** chopped		3/4 cup
1 tsp.	**Yeast** fast rise		2 tsp.
	- or -		
2 tsp.	**Yeast** active dry		3 tsp.

This is bread with the jam already inside. It's a coffee bread, a snack bread or the perfect after-school bread. This finely textured sweet bread also happens to be lovely, with the summery orange apricots floating in the golden loaf.

Success Hints

- Crust may brown more because of the sugar. If your machine offers the option, use the "light" crust feature.

- We use dried apricots preserved without sulflur dioxide. This preservative sometimes de-activates the yeast.

- Use a jam with a high fruit content and few other additives.

- This recipe can be baked with the regular, rapid, or delayed time bake cycles.

Pumpernickel

Calories 146   Protein 11 %
Cholesterol 4.52 mg.   Carbohydrates 75 %
Sodium 247 mg.   Fat 14 %

Nutritional information per serving

This heavy, dark bread is a traditional pumpernickel - the kind that will leave you reaching for smoked salmon and cream cheese. The loaf is shorter and denser than most because of the heavy flours, which call for an extra knead. With bread machines, that simply means one extra button to push - not too much to ask for a loaf this fresh and this rich.

Success Hints

- Remember the extra knead. The whole wheat and rye flours used in this recipe are low in gluten. To overcome this, after the machine has completed its first knead, simply reset and restart the machine.

- It's not unusual for the top to be slightly honey-combed.

- Because of the double knead, we use this recipe only on the regular bake cycle.

regular loaf		large loaf
3/4 cup	Water	1 1/4 cups
1 cup	White Bread Flour	1 1/2 cups
1/3 cup	Wheat Bread Flour	1/2 cup
2/3 cup	Rye Flour	1 cup
1 Tbsp.	Dry Milk	1 1/2 Tbsp.
1 1/4 Tbsp.	Sugar	2 Tbsp.
1 tsp.	Salt	1 1/2 tsp.
1 1/4 Tbsp.	Butter	2 Tbsp.
2 Tbsp.	Cornmeal	1/4 cup
1 Tbsp. + 2 tsp.	Cocoa powdered	2 1/2 Tbsp.
2 1/2 Tbsp.	Molasses	3 1/2 Tbsp.
1/4 tsp.	Instant Coffee	1/2 tsp.
1 tsp.	Caraway Seeds	2 tsp.
1 2/3 tsp.	Yeast fast rise	2 1/2 tsp.
	- or -	
2 1/2 tsp.	Yeast active dry	3 1/4 tsp.

Onion

Calories 161   Protein 12 %
Cholesterol 4.89 mg.   Carbohydrates 75 %
Sodium 268 mg.   Fat 13 %

Nutritional information per serving

Mary Ann says that when she was baking this bread in the test kitchen, folks would come in off the streets asking, "What *is* this place?" The aroma has that kind of effect, so does the taste. Serve it warm with split pea soup, and your senses will think they've died and gone to heaven.

Success Hints

■ Use dried onion flakes, not fresh.

■ Old onion bread makes marvelous croutons and bread crumbs. See recipe on page 26.

■ If you can't find onion paste in a tube, you may substitute onion powder. Substitue 1/4 tsp. for the regular loaf and 1/3 tsp. for the large. Onion salt will not work.

■ This recipe can be baked with the regular or rapid bake cycles.

regular loaf		large loaf
3/4 cup	**Water**	1 1/4 cup
2 cups	**White Bread Flour**	3 1/4 cups
1 1/2 Tbsp.	**Dry Milk**	2 Tbsp.
1 1/2 Tbsp.	**Brown Sugar**	2 Tbsp.
1 tsp.	**Salt**	1 1/2 tsp.
1 Tbsp.	**Butter**	2 Tbsp.
1/4 cup	**Onions** *dried*	1/2 cup
1/2 Tbsp.	**Onion Paste**	1 Tbsp.
1/2 tsp.	**Black Pepper**	1 tsp.
1/2 tsp.	**Poppy Seeds**	1 tsp.
1 tsp.	**Yeast** *fast rise*	1 1/2 tsp.
	- or -	
2 tsp.	**Yeast** *active dry*	3 tsp.

Rum Raisin

Calories 226   Protein 10 %
Cholesterol 2.84 mg. Carbohydrates 69 %
Sodium 301 mg.   Fat 21 %

Nutritional information per serving

Rum Raisin is another one of those versatile breads that can stretch from breakfast to dessert. Sweeter and richer than our standard raisin bread, Rum Raisin is subtle enough not to be overwhelming while rich enough to stand out. Serve it with our Honey Butter spread for a real treat.

Success Hints

- Soak raisins in spicy rum overnight and drain before using.

- Measure raisins after they have soaked.

- For additional rum flavor add 1/4 teaspoon rum extract. For a non-alcoholic version, pre-soak the raisins in water and use rum extract.

- This recipe can be baked with the regular or rapid bake cycles.

regular loaf		large loaf
1/2 cup	**Water**	3/4 cup
2 cups	**White Bread Flour**	3 cups
1 Tbsp.	**Dry Milk**	2 Tbsp.
2 tsp.	**Brown Sugar**	1 Tbsp.
1 tsp.	**Salt**	1 1/2 tsp.
2 tsp.	**Butter**	1 Tbsp.
1/2 cup	**Raisins** *pre-soaked in rum*	3/4 cup
2 Tbsp.	**Heavy Cream**	1/4 cup
1	**Egg** *beaten*	1
1 tsp.	**Olive Oil**	1 Tbsp.
3/4 tsp.	**Yeast** *fast rise*	1 1/8 tsp.
	- or -	
1 1/2 tsp.	**Yeast** *active dry*	2 tsp.

Luscious Luau

Calories 226   Protein 9 %
Cholesterol 4.89 mg. Carbohydrates 61 %
Sodium 278 mg.   Fat 30 %

Nutritional information per serving

One bite of this light, sweet loaf and you can feel the tropical breezes. The pineapple and coconut add sweetness and flavor, but the macadamia nuts are the real stars of the show. This is one bread that's better served cool than hot. The pineapple is especially enhanced with cooling. The possibilities for this bread are endless, but we'll tell you this: Luscious Luau makes toast a celestial experience.

Success Hints

■ Drain the pineapple well.

■ Macadamia nuts add a wonderful texture if added in large chunks. We quarter ours.

■ For extra flavor, reserved pineapple juice may be substituted for up to 2/3 of the water.

■ This recipe can be baked with the regular and rapid bake cycles.

regular loaf		large loaf
3/4 cup	**Water**	1 cup
2 1/3 cups	**White Bread Flour**	3 1/2 cups
1 Tbsp.	**Dry Milk**	2 Tbsp.
1 tsp.	**Salt**	1 1/2 tsp.
1 Tbsp.	**Butter**	2 Tbsp.
1 1/2 Tbsp.	**Brown Sugar**	2 Tbsp.
2 Tbsp.	**Carrots** shredded	1/4 cup
1/4 cup	**Coconut** flaked/shredded	1/2 cup
1/2 cup	**Pineapple** unsweetened crushed	3/4 cup
1/3 cup	**Macadamia Nuts** coarsely chopped	1/2 cup
pinch	**Cinnamon**	1/8 tsp.
1 tsp.	**Yeast** fast rise	2 tsp.
	- or -	
2 tsp.	**Yeast** active dry	3 tsp.

Pizza Pleasure

Calories 211   Protein 16 %
Cholesterol 11.7 mg. Carbohydrates 53 %
Sodium 501 mg.   Fat 31 %

Nutritional information per serving

In the wintertime, Suzan's son, Martin, likes to have "pizza picnics" on a picnic blanket in front of the fireplace. With this bread, you can take your pizza on a real picnic - it's that close to the real thing. Just toss a loaf in your picnic basket, and you're ready to go. Finally, pizza with a perfect crust!

Success Hints

- Use stick pepperoni and dice into 1/4" chunks.

- As with all cheese breads, loaf appearance will be unusual due to the moisture of the cheese - a small price to pay for great taste.

- This bread can be made with the regular and rapid bake cycles.

regular loaf		large loaf
3/4 cup	**Water**	1 3/8 cup
2 cups	**White Bread Flour**	3 cups
1 Tbsp.	**Dry Milk**	2 Tbsp.
1 Tbsp.	**Sugar**	2 Tbsp.
1 tsp.	**Salt**	1 1/2 tsp.
1 Tbsp.	**Butter**	2 Tbsp.
1/3 cup	**Pepperoni** *chopped*	1/2 cup
1/4 cup	**Mozzarella** *shredded*	1/3 cup
2 tsp.	**Parmesan** *grated*	1 Tbsp.
1/4 cup	**Mushrooms** *canned/drained*	1/3 cup
2 Tbsp.	**Onion Flakes**	1/4 cup
1/2 tsp.	**Garlic Powder**	3/4 tsp.
1/2 tsp.	**Oregano**	3/4 tsp.
1 tsp.	**Yeast** *fast rise*	1 1/2 tsp.
	- or -	
2 tsp.	**Yeast** *active dry*	2 1/2 tsp.

Peaches and Cream

Calories 162   Protein 12 %
Cholesterol 0.47 mg. Carbohydrates 84 %
Sodium 215 mg.   Fat 4 %

Nutritional information per serving

You may love your peaches and cream chilled, but the way to serve this lovely light bread is warm from the oven. Like your favorite peach cobbler, the subtle richness of the flavors lends itself perfectly to a light topping of fresh butter. Try it for bread and butter sandwiches and you may decide to make afternoon tea a ritual.

Success Hints

- For a creamy texture, use low fat yogurt; if you're calorie counting, nonfat will do.

- For more of a cobbler effect, increase nutmeg and cinnamon to taste.

- This bread tends to have a dark crust. Try the "light" crust setting.

- This recipe can be used with the regular and quick bake cycles.

regular loaf		large loaf
1/2 cup	Water	3/4 cup
2 cups	White Bread Flour	3 cups
1 Tbsp.	Dry Milk	1 1/2 Tbsp.
2 tsp.	Brown Sugar	1 Tbsp.
3/4 tsp.	Salt	1 1/4 tsp.
1/2 cup	Dried Peaches *coarsely diced*	3/4 cup
1/3 cup	Peach Yogurt	1/2 cup
2 Tbsp.	Applesauce	1/4 cup
1/8 tsp.	Nutmeg	1/4 tsp.
1/8 tsp.	Cinnamon	1/4 tsp.
1 1/2 tsp.	Yeast *fast rise*	2 tsp.
	- or -	
2 tsp.	Yeast *active dry*	3 tsp.

Nutty Coconut

Calories 191   Protein 10 %
Cholesterol 3.9 mg.   Carbohydrates 59 %
Sodium 288 mg.   Fat 31 %

Nutritional information per serving

This softly subtle bread has a wonderful chewy texture. The coconut, pecans and walnuts make a harmonious trio in morning toast. Or serve this bread freshly baked as an accompaniment to your favorite fruit salad.

regular loaf		large loaf
3/4 cup	**Water**	1 1/8 cups
2 cups	**White Bread Flour**	3 cups
1 tsp.	**Salt**	1 1/2 tsp.
1 Tbsp.	**Butter**	1 1/2 Tbsp.
1 Tbsp.	**Cream of Coconut** canned	2 Tbsp.
1/4 cup	**Coconut** flaked or shredded	1/2 cup
3 Tbsp.	**Pecans**	1/4 cup
3 Tbsp.	**Walnuts**	1/4 cup
1 tsp.	**Yeast** fast rise	2 tsp.
	- or -	
2 tsp.	**Yeast** active dry	3 tsp.

Success Hints

■ For optimal flavor, use pure canned coconut milk instead of the water-added variety.

■ For additional chewy crunch, use shredded coconut.

■ This recipe can be made with the regular or rapid bake cycles.

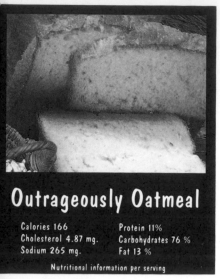

regular loaf		large loaf
3/4 cup	**Water**	1 1/4 cups
2 cups	**White Bread Flour**	3 cups
1 Tbsp.	**Dry Milk**	1 1/2 Tbsp.
1 tsp.	**Salt**	1 1/2 tsp.
1 Tbsp.	**Butter**	2 Tbsp.
1 Tbsp.	**Honey**	2 Tbsp.
1/4 cup	**Rolled Oats**	1/2 cup
1 tsp.	**Yeast** *fast rise*	2 tsp.
	- or -	
1 1/2 tsp.	**Yeast** *active dry*	3 tsp.

Outrageously Oatmeal

Calories 166   Protein 11%
Cholesterol 4.87 mg.   Carbohydrates 76 %
Sodium 265 mg.   Fat 13 %

Nutritional information per serving

There's more than one way to eat your oatmeal. One taste of this full-bodied white bread, and you'll never call it mush again! The light oat taste makes it a natural for hearty morning toast. This nicely textured bread makes fine sandwiches, too.

Success Hints

- For added texture, add the oats after the first knead or at the beep on the fruit and nut cycle.

- For additional crunch, sprinkle a few oats on top of the loaf after the final rise.

- Instant oatmeal doesn't work, but quick-cooking oats do.

- Try with Ginger Pecan Butter - page 143.

- This recipe can be made with the regular, rapid, or delayed time bake cycles.

Chocolate Cherry

Calories 192   Protein 10 %
Cholesterol 0.12 mg. Carbohydrates 76 %
Sodium 280 mg.   Fat 14 %

Nutritional information per serving

You'll never have to ask the kids to finish their bread again. Paul Swalling, 10 years old, visited the test kitchen and managed to eat a whole loaf before anyone noticed! For adults, Chocolate Cherry turns a coffee break into a pleasant interlude. With a sweet topping, it becomes a new dessert bread.

Success Hints

- Make sure to use real chocolate chips.

- Dried Chukar brand cherries are available in our accessories section. You may use either dried bing or dried tart red cherries in this recipe.

- This recipe can be made with the regular, rapid, or delayed time bake cycles.

regular loaf		large loaf
3/4 cup	**Water**	1 1/4 cup
1 1/2 cups	**White Bread Flour**	2 cups
1/2 cup	**Wheat Bread Flour**	1 cup
1 Tbsp.	**Dry Milk**	2 Tbsp.
2 Tbsp.	**Molasses**	1/4 cup
1 tsp.	**Salt**	1 1/2 tsp.
1/3 cup	**Chocolate Chips**	1/2 cup
1/3 cup	**Cherries** *dried*	1/2 cup
2 tsp.	**Triple Sec** *liqueur*	1 Tbsp.
1/4 tsp.	**Orange Peel**	1/2 tsp.
1 tsp.	**Yeast** *fast rise*	2 tsp.
	- or -	
2 tsp.	**Yeast** *active dry*	3 tsp.

Fall Harvest

Calories 155   Protein 12 %
Cholesterol 4.89 mg.   Carbohydrates 73 %
Sodium 267 mg.   Fat 15 %

Nutritional information per serving

We originally called this Pumpkin Bread but decided that was too suggestive of pumpkin pie. Rather than sweet, this loaf is a full-bodied squash bread, more reminiscent of acorn squash. The pumpkin seeds are a wonderful, distinctive touch; they give the bread crunch along with a special taste of autumn.

Success Hints

- Be sure to use plain canned pumpkin - not pumpkin pie filling.

- This recipe can be made with the regular and rapid bake cycles.

regular loaf		large loaf
1/2 cup	**Water**	1 cup
2 cups	**White Bread Flour**	3 cups
1 Tbsp.	**Dry Milk**	2 Tbsp.
1 tsp.	**Salt**	1 1/2 tsp.
1 Tbsp.	**Butter**	2 Tbsp.
1/2 Tbsp.	**Maple Syrup**	1 Tbsp.
1/2 Tbsp.	**Brown Sugar**	1/2 Tbsp.
1/4 cup	**Pumpkin** canned	1/2 cup
1/2 tsp.	**Vanilla Extract**	1 tsp.
1/2 tsp.	**Ginger** ground	3/4 tsp.
1/4 tsp.	**Allspice**	1/2 tsp.
1/4 cup	**Pumpkin Seeds**	1/2 cup
1 tsp.	**Yeast** fast rise	1 1/2 tsp.
	- or -	
2 tsp.	**Yeast** active dry	3 tsp.

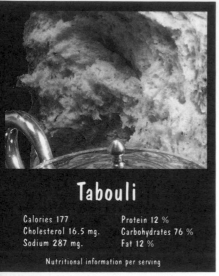

Tabouli

Calories 177
Cholesterol 16.5 mg.
Sodium 287 mg.
Protein 12 %
Carbohydrates 76 %
Fat 12 %

Nutritional information per serving

This is a bread that's definitely different. Inspired by the Middle Eastern bulgur wheat dish, this medium bodied loaf offers a unique blending of tastes and textures. Mary, a tabouli lover, says it can't be beat for a meatloaf sandwich. Or try it with a Greek salad or slices of warm feta cheese.

Success Hints

- For additional flavor, add 1/2 tsp. of dried mint leaves.

- Place apricots away from water.

- Tabouli mix can be found in the gourmet or health food section of your grocery.

- This recipe can be made with the regular or rapid bake cycles.

regular loaf		large loaf
1/2 cup	**Water**	1 cup
2 cups	**White Bread Flour**	3 1/4 cups
1 Tbsp.	**Sugar**	2 Tbsp.
3/4 tsp.	**Salt**	1 1/2 tsp.
1	**Egg**	1
2 Tbsp.	**Apricots** chopped/dried	1/4 cup
2 Tbsp.	**Black Olives** chopped	1/4 cup
1/2 Tbsp.	**Olive Oil**	1 Tbsp.
1/4 cup	**Tabouli Mix**	1/2 cup
2 Tbsp.	**Yogurt**	1/4 cup
1 tsp.	**Yeast** fast rise	2 tsp.
	- or -	
2 tsp.	**Yeast** active dry	3 tsp.

Greek Isle

Calories 142   Protein 14 %
Cholesterol 7.87 mg.   Carbohydrates 69 %
Sodium 318 mg.   Fat 17 %

Nutritional information per serving

Unique is the word for this loaf. Don't let the combination of ingredients scare you off - the texture created by the feta cheese combined with the smallest hint of cucumber makes this a wonderful bread. This is definitely a bread to accompany a hot meal. We recommend it with char-grilled marinated lamb chops or your favorite lamb kabobs.

Success Hints

- Cucumber should be peeled, seeded and then pureed.

- If the feta cheese is packed in water, drain well.

- Finely chop black olives.

- The recipe can be made with the regular and rapid bake cycles.

regular loaf		large loaf
1/2 cup	**Water**	3/4 cup
2 cups	**White Bread Flour**	3 cups
3 Tbsp.	**Yogurt** *plain*	1/4 cup
2 tsp.	**Dry Milk**	1 Tbsp.
1 Tbsp.	**Sugar**	1 1/2 Tbsp.
1 tsp.	**Salt**	1 1/2 tsp.
2 tsp.	**Butter**	1 Tbsp.
pinch	**Garlic Powder**	1/4 tsp.
4 tsp.	**Black Olives** *chopped*	2 Tbsp.
1/2 tsp.	**Sweet Basil**	3/4 tsp.
1/2 tsp.	**Dill Weed**	3/4 tsp.
2 1/2 Tbsp.	**Feta Cheese**	1/4 cup
2 1/2 Tbsp.	**Cucumber** *pureed*	1/4 cup
1/2 tsp.	**Yeast** *fast rise*	3/4 tsp.
	- or -	
1 tsp.	**Yeast** *active dry*	1 1/2 tsp.

Sun Nut

Calories 187 Protein 12 %
Cholesterol 5.3 mg. Carbohydrates 64 %
Sodium 111 mg. Fat 24 %

Nutritional information per serving

This is a bread to make sunflower lovers sing. The sunflower seeds impart a lovely, subtle taste and a lovely chewy texture. Toasted, this bread does wonderful things with fruit and jelly, and it will breathe new life into that predictable cheese sandwich.

Success Hints

- If using unsalted sunflower seeds, increase the salt by a pinch.

- This bread makes croutons with a new kind of crunch. See our low fat recipe on page 26.

- Sunflower seed salt content varies by brand. If using low or unsalted seeds, adjust salt accordingly.

- This recipe can be made with the regular, rapid, or delayed time bake cycles.

regular loaf		large loaf
3/4 cup	**Water**	1 1/4 cups
1 3/4 cups	**White Bread Flour**	2 1/2 cups
1/2 cup	**Wheat Bread Flour**	3/4 cup
1 Tbsp.	**Dry Milk**	2 Tbsp.
1/4 tsp.	**Salt**	1/2 tsp.
1 Tbsp.	**Butter**	2 Tbsp.
2 Tbsp.	**Honey**	3 Tbsp.
1/4 cup	**Sunflower Seeds**	1/2 cup
1 1/4 tsp.	**Yeast** *fast rise*	2 tsp.
	- or -	
2 tsp.	**Yeast** *active dry*	3 tsp.

Bleu Cheese & Port

Calories 170   Protein 12 %
Cholesterol 2.56 mg. Carbohydrates 70 %
Sodium 276 mg.   Fat 18 %

Nutritional information per serving

regular loaf		large loaf
2/3 cup	**Water**	1 cup
2 cups	**White Bread Flour**	3 cups
1 Tbsp.	**Sugar**	2 Tbsp.
1 tsp.	**Salt**	1 1/2 tsp.
2 tsp.	**Butter**	1 Tbsp.
2 Tbsp.	**Port Red Wine**	1/4 cup
1/4 cup	**Blue Cheese**	1/3 cup
1/4 cup	**Walnuts** *coarsely chopped*	1/3 cup
2 1/2 Tbsp.	**Applesauce**	1/4 cup
3/4 tsp.	**Yeast** *fast rise*	1 tsp.
	- or -	
1 1/2 tsp.	**Yeast** *active dry*	2 tsp.

Whether bleu or blue, there are no two ways about it - a blue cheese lover will love this bread. This moderately textured loaf makes great croutons and wonderful toast points for parties. Or serve it warm with your favorite steak.

Success Hints

- No need to use an expensive port here, just one with good flavor.

- The sharper the blue cheese, the stronger the flavor in the bread. We like the Danish blue best.

- As with all cheese recipes, loaf appearance may vary but the flavor is worth it.

- This recipe can be made with the regular and rapid bake cycles.

Sourdough White

Calories 166   Protein 12 %
Cholesterol 5.78 mg. Carbohydrates 75 %
Sodium 313 mg.   Fat 13 %

Nutritional information per serving

regular loaf		large loaf
1 1/2 cup	**Starter**	2 cup
1 1/2 cups	**White Bread Flour**	2 cups
1 Tbsp.	**Dry Milk**	2 Tbps.
1 Tbsp.	**Sugar**	2 Tbsp.
1 tsp.	**Salt**	1 1/2 tsp.
1 Tbsp.	**Butter**	2 Tbsp.
1 tsp.	**Yeast** *fast rise optional*	2 tsp.
	- or -	
2 tsp.	**Yeast** *active dry optional*	3 tsp.

If you're in the pioneering spirit, here's a Sourdough for you. Yes, sourdough *is* possible in a bread machine - for bakers with the time, patience and adventuresome spirit to see this most independent bread to completion. Because every starter is different, sourdough baking is always a challenge. In bread machines, it becomes its own art form. Experiment - it's the hallmark of a Sourdough baker!

Success Hints

- Follow preparation instructions for your chosen starter. Starter may take 24 hours to 4 days to activate.

- To ensure proper balance, always feed your starter equal parts flour and water (85°).

- We baked our Sourdough successes on the regular cycle.

- Sourdough starters are formulated from wild yeasts. Sourdough purists may omit the yeast listed above. Note: the more active the starter, the less yeast you'll need.

- Timing and temperature are the key elements of success.
    * Careful observation will reveal your starter's peaking schedule. Starter should be peaking when loaded into machine, frothy and bubbly, not just foamy.
    * Optimum room temperature for culture activation and machine baking is 85°.

- If starter peaks at an inconvenient time, store it in the refrigerator. Re-activate by feeding again and placing in an 85-95° place for 6-12 hours.

- Save some of the active starter for your next batch. Refrigerate in an airtight container.

- We used the variety of different starters available in our accessories section.

Banana Granola

This is a fairly heavy, moist bread that's not as sweet as the ingredients might suggest. The fruit and granola combine to make a slightly nutty taste with a hint of banana. This bread makes terrific toast with a hearty breakfast of bacon and eggs.

Success Hints

- Mash bananas well or use a food processor.

- Measure the bananas after mashing.

- This bread is wonderful with the Honey Butter - page 143.

- Use your favorite granola mix for your own personalized flavor.

- This recipe can be made with the regular or rapid bake cycles.

regular loaf		large loaf
2/3 cup	**Water**	1 cup
1 1/4 cups	**White Bread Flour**	2 cups
3/4 cup	**Wheat Bread Flour**	1 cup
4 tsp.	**Dry Milk**	2 Tbsp.
1 tsp.	**Salt**	1 1/2 tsp.
4 tsp.	**Butter**	2 Tbsp.
1/2 cup	**Bananas** *mashed*	1/2 cup
1/2 cup	**Granola**	3/4 cup
4 tsp.	**Molasses**	1/4 cup
1/4 cup	**Walnuts** *chopped*	1/3 cup
1/4 cup	**Banana Chips** *dried*	1/3 cup
1 tsp.	**Yeast** *fast rise*	2 tsp.
	- or -	
1 1/2 tsp.	**Yeast** *active dry*	3 tsp.

Tangy Cranberry

Calories 182   Protein 10 %
Cholesterol 5.3 mg.   Carbohydrates 78 %
Sodium 289 mg.   Fat 12 %

Nutritional information per serving

Wanna bet there's nothing new to do with that leftover turkey? This moist, light bread promises to redefine your idea of a turkey sandwich. But don't stop there. Try a slice of sharp cheddar with a little English mustard. Experiment - and enjoy.

regular loaf		large loaf
3/4 cup	**Cranberry Juice**	1 1/4 cup
2 cups	**White Bread Flour**	3 cups
1 Tbsp.	**Dry Milk**	2 Tbsp.
1 tsp.	**Salt**	1 1/2 tsp.
1 Tbsp.	**Butter**	2 Tbsp.
1/4 cup	**Cranberries** *dried*	1/3 cup
2 Tbsp.	**Orange Marmalade**	3 Tbsp.
1 tsp.	**Yeast** *fast rise*	2 tsp.
	- or -	
2 tsp.	**Yeast** *active dry*	3 tsp.

Success Hints

- Chukar brand dried cranberries are available in our accessories section. Gourmet stores and specialty food catalogs also carry dried cranberries.

- Place dried cranberries away from water if baking on delayed time cycle.

- This recipe can be baked with regular or delayed time bake cycles.

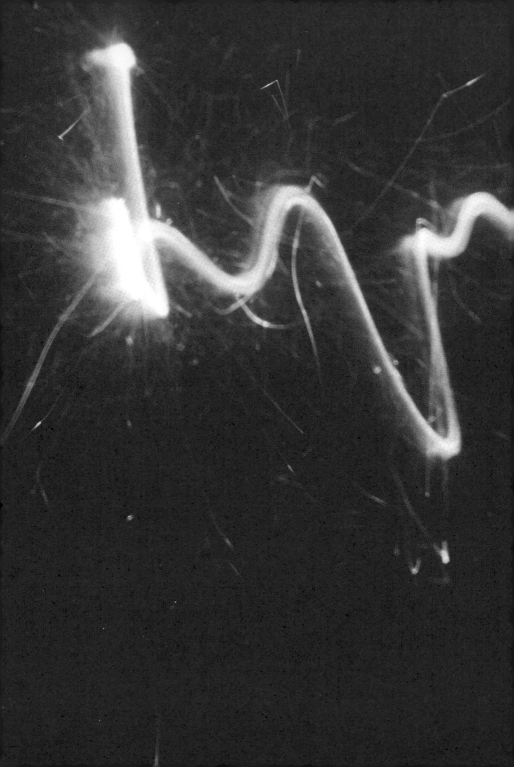

SPECIALTY BREADS

These festive recipes combine the
ease of machine preparation with
the satisfying creativity of baking.
Your machine mixes and kneads
the dough, then you form it and
bake it in your regular oven.
Surprise your friends with new
shapes of electric bread!

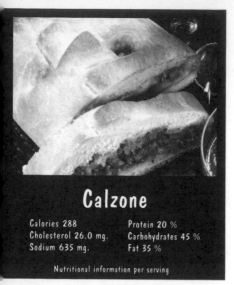

Calzone

Calories 288
Cholesterol 26.0 mg.
Sodium 635 mg.
Protein 20 %
Carbohydrates 45 %
Fat 35 %

Nutritional information per serving

	regular loaf		large loaf
3/4 cup	**Water**		1 1/4 cups
2 cups	**White Bread Flour**		3 cups
1/2 tsp.	**Dry Milk**		1 tsp.
1 Tbsp.	**Sugar**		1 1/2 Tbsp.
1/2 tsp.	**Salt**		1 tsp.
1 tsp.	**Yeast** *fast rise*		2 tsp.
	- or -		
2 tsp.	**Yeast** *active dry*		3 tsp.

Remove dough from the machine after the dough or manual cycle is completed, then follow the process steps.

Think of Calzone as an elegant alternative to pizza. Your choice of fillings is limited only by your imagination; dress it up for a buffet or make it a simple one course family meal.

Success Hints

- Calzone can be prepared several hours ahead of time and kept in the refrigerator until baking time.

- Double the pizza sauce recipe and drizzle warm sauce over the Calzone before serving.

- Add pesto to pizza sauce if you like extra garlic and basil.

FILLING		
1/2 cup	**Pizza Sauce**	3/4 cup
1/2 cup	**Italian Sausage** *sweet*	3/4 cup
1 cup	**Mozzarella Cheese** *shredded*	1 1/4 cup
sprinkle	**Feta Cheese, Pepperoni, Green Peppers, Onions, Olives** *chopped*	sprinkle

Roll out on a lightly floured surface to a 16 x 10 rectangle for a large loaf, or a 12 x 8 for a regular loaf. Transfer to lightly greased cookie sheet. Spoon pizza sauce onto center of dough, and add filling. Make diagonal cuts 1 1/2 inches apart down each side, cutting to within a half inch of the filling. Crisscross strips of dough over filling, pressing down and sealing with a drop of water. Brush top with melted butter and bake at 350° 35-45 minutes until golden brown.

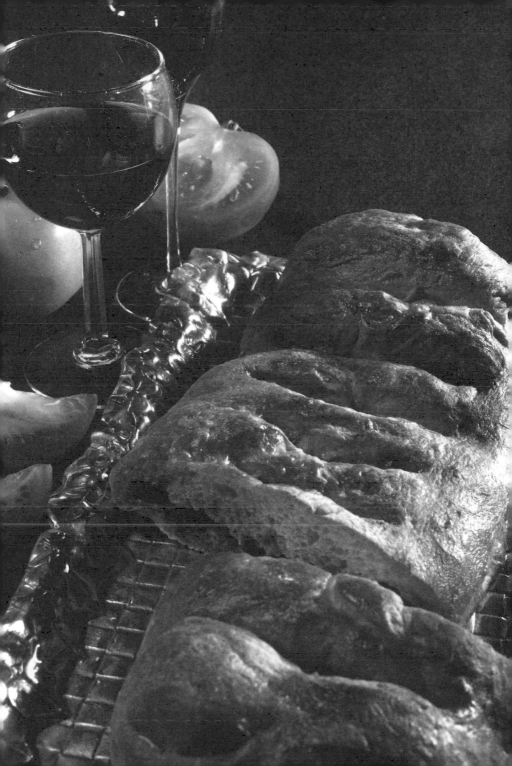

Honey-Bran English Muffins

Calories 168   Protein 11 %
Cholesterol 5.18 mg.   Carbohydrates 76 %
Sodium 106 mg.   Fat 13 %

Nutritional information per serving

Slightly sweet and nutty, these English muffins stick to your ribs without being too heavy. Try them toasted with our Guava-Raisin spread on page 143.

regular loaf		large loaf
3/4 cup	**Water**	1 1/4 cups
2 cups	**White Bread Flour**	3 cups
1/4 tsp.	**Salt**	1/2 tsp.
1 Tbsp.	**Butter**	2 Tbsp.
2 Tbsp.	**Honey**	3 Tbsp.
1/2 cup	**Wheat Bran** cereal bits	3/4 cup
1 tsp.	**Yeast** fast rise	2 tsp.
	- or -	
2 tsp.	**Yeast** active dry	3 tsp.
1 Tbsp.	**Oat Bran**	1 1/2 Tbsp.

Remove dough from the machine after the dough or manual cycle is completed, then follow the process steps.

Turn dough out onto floured surface. Divide into 12 portions for large loaf, 8 for regular. Shape each into a ball, then press into 4" circles about 3/4" high. Grease baking sheet and sprinkle with half the oat bran, then place muffins 2" apart. Spritz with water and sprinkle with remaining bran. Let rise until doubled, about an hour. Grease electric skillet or griddle and preheat to 340° or medium heat. Carefully place muffins in skillet, then cook about 6 minutes on each side or until brown. Cool.

Saffron Braids

Calories 164   Protein 13 %
Cholesterol 18.6 mg.   Carbohydrates 69 %
Sodium 288 mg.   Fat 18 %

Nutritional information per serving

		regular loaf		large loaf

regular loaf		large loaf
3/4 cup	**Water**	1 1/4 cups
2 cups	**White Bread Flour**	3 cups
1 tsp.	**Sugar**	1/2 Tbsp.
1 tsp.	**Salt**	1 1/2 tsp.
1	**Egg**	1
1 1/2 Tbsp.	**Olive Oil**	2 Tbsp.
1/4 tsp.	**Saffron** ground	1/2 tsp.
	-or-	
1/8 tsp.	**Saffron** hair	1/4 tsp.
1 tsp.	**Yeast** fast rise	2 tsp.
	- or -	
2 tsp.	**Yeast** active dry	3 tsp.

As beautiful as it is exotic, this bread is a genuinely unique addition to any dinner party. Because the dough is prepared in the machine, this succulent centerpiece takes surprisingly little time to prepare.

Success Hints

■ If using saffron hair, grind with mortar and pestle. It does not need to be a fine powder.

Remove dough from the machine after the dough or manual cycle is completed, then follow the process steps.

Turn dough out onto floured surface (it will be sticky) and punch down. Divide and make three ropes about 9 - 12 " long, depending on loaf size. Pinch ropes together at one end, braid, and pinch together at other end to secure braid. Transfer to greased baking sheet, let rise until double in size (about one hour). Brush with beaten egg and sprinkle with sesame seeds. Bake at 375° for 20-25 minutes.

Fruit Spiral

Calories 270
Cholesterol 32.1 mg.
Sodium 239 mg.

Protein 10 %
Carbohydrates 61 %
Fat 29 %

Nutritional information per serving

This festive brunch offering takes a little time - but not nearly as much as your guests will think! The crushed sugar cubes give a wonderful crunch to the topping.

regular loaf		large loaf
3/4 cup	**Water**	1 1/4 cups
2 cups	**White Bread Flour**	3 cups
1 Tbsp.	**Dry Milk**	2 Tbsp.
1 1/2 Tbsp.	**Sugar**	2 Tbsp.
1/2 tsp.	**Salt**	1 tsp.
1 1/2 Tbsp.	**Butter**	2 Tbsp.
1	**Egg**	1
3/4 tsp.	**Coriander** ground	1 tsp.
1 1/2 tsp.	**Lemon Peel** dried	1/2 Tbsp.
1 tsp.	**Yeast** fast rise	2 tsp.
	- or -	
2 tsp.	**Yeast** active dry	3 tsp.

FILLING

3 Tbsp.	**Brown Sugar**	1/4 cup	1/4 cup	**Almond Paste**	1/2 cup
1/2 cup	**Apricots** dried	1 cup	2 Tbsp.	**Butter**	3 1/2 Tbsp.
1/2 cup	**Apples** dried & diced	1 cup	2 Tbsp.	**Sugar Cubes** crushed	3 1/2 Tbsp.

Turn dough out onto lightly floured surface and punch down. Roll and stretch dough into thin strip, 5 - 6" wide and 36" long for large loaf, 3 - 5" wide and 27" long for regular loaf. Keep board floured. Dot strip with butter and filling ingredients. Brush edge with water, fold over into a tube, sealing ingredients inside. Coiling from one end, form 5 - 7" circle with seam inside. Coil remaining dough, gradually spiraling narrower and higher. Transfer to greased baking sheet and let rise until double, about one hour. Brush with beaten egg, sprinkle with crushed sugar cubes. Bake at 325° for 30 minutes. To prevent over-browning, cover with foil and continue baking for 20 minutes more.

Orange Kisses

Calories 299　　　Protein 6 %
Cholesterol 28.5 mg.　Carbohydrates 61 %
Sodium 270 mg.　　Fat 33 %

Nutritional information per serving

Ann's mother, Wanda Thompson, used to make these festive fruit rolls for holidays. For years, Ann "cheated" with time-saving frozen bread dough to imitate her mother's recipe. Now Ann uses her bread machine to pass the tradition along to her daughters. The sugar bakes with the orange rind and butter to create a crispy, crunchy top - and a decadently gooey bottom.

regular loaf		large loaf
3/4 cup	**Water**	1 1/4 cups
2 cups	**White Bread Flour**	3 cups
1/2 Tbsp.	**Orange Peel** *dried*	1 Tbsp.
1 1/2 Tbsp.	**Dry Milk**	2 Tbsp.
2 Tbsp.	**Sugar**	3 Tbsp.
1/2 tsp.	**Salt**	1 tsp.
2 Tbsp.	**Butter**	3 Tbsp.
1 tsp.	**Yeast** *fast rise*	2 tsp.
	- or -	
2 tsp.	**Yeast** *active dry*	3 tsp.

Remove dough from the machine after the dough or manual cycle is completed, then follow the process steps.

COATING		
1/2 cup	**Butter** *softened*	1/2 cup
1 1/2 Tbsp.	**Orange Rind** *fresh grated*	3 Tbsp.
1/2 cup	**Sugar**	1 cup

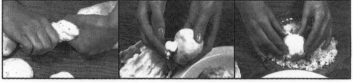

Turn dough out onto a lightly floured surface. Divide large loaf into 12 portions, and 8 for the regular loaf. Form into balls, and coat each ball with softened butter. Roll in orange-sugar mixture. Place in 10" pan for large loaf, 8" for regular. Let rise until dough doubles, about one hour. Bake at 350° 25-30 minutes until just golden brown.

Sticky Buns

Calories 321
Cholesterol 28.6 mg.
Sodium 279 mg.
Protein 6 %
Carbohydrates 54 %
Fat 40 %

Nutritional information per serving

regular loaf		large loaf
3/4 cup	**Water**	1 1/4 cups
2 cups	**White Bread Flour**	3 cups
1 1/2 Tbsp.	**Dry Milk**	2 Tbsp.
2 Tbsp.	**Sugar**	3 Tbsp.
1/2 tsp.	**Salt**	1 tsp.
2 Tbsp.	**Butter**	3 Tbsp.
1 tsp.	**Yeast** *fast rise*	2 tsp.
	- or -	
2 tsp.	**Yeast** *active dry*	3 tsp.

Is there anything like homemade sticky buns? Kids love to help roll out the dough and add the nuts. Let it become one of *their* specialities!

Remove dough from the machine after the dough or manual cycle is completed, then follow the process steps.

STICKY SAUCE

1/4 cup	**Butter**	1/4 cup
1/2 cup	**Brown Sugar**	1/2 cup
1/4 cup	**Corn Syrup** *light*	1/4 cup
1/4 cup	**Pecans** *broken*	1/2 cup

Warm over medium heat until sugar dissolves.

FILLING

1/4 cup	**Soft Butter**	1/3 cup
1/2 tsp.	**Cinnamon**	1 tsp.

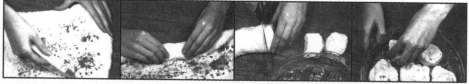

Prepare sticky sauce and pour into 13 x 9 pan for large and 8 x 8 for regular loaf. Sprinkle with broken nuts. Turn dough out onto floured surface (it will be sticky), and punch down. Roll dough to a 16 x 10 rectangle for large loaf, 12 x 8 for regular. Dot with soft butter and sprinkle with cinnamon. Roll jellyroll style and pinch seams together. Slice 1 1/2" thick pieces, place into pan on top of sticky sauce, and let double in size (about one hour). Bake at 375° for 20-25 minutes. Cool for no more than three minutes, then invert pan so sauce and nuts are on top of buns.

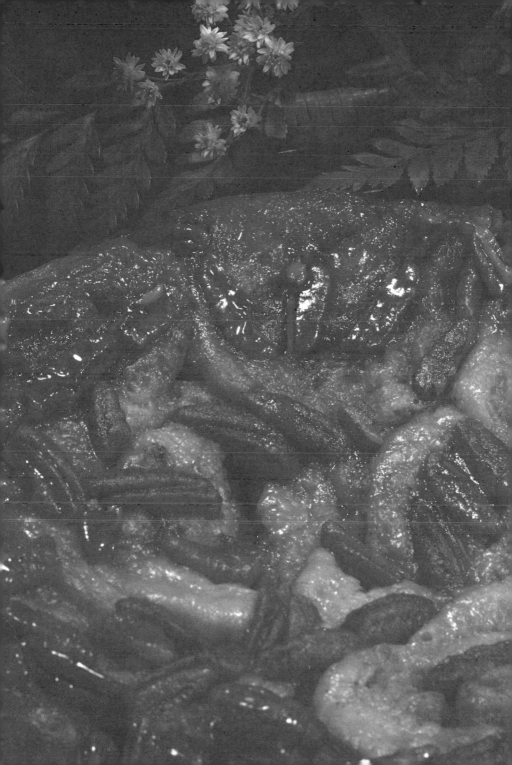

Pepper Jack Ties

Calories 188   Protein 17 %
Cholesterol 12.5 mg.   Carbohydrates 60 %
Sodium 256 mg.   Fat 23 %

Nutritional information per serving

These are dinner rolls with a difference - a little kick and a whole lot of flavor. They're best served warm.

regular loaf		large loaf
3/4 cup	**Water**	1 1/4 cups
2 cups	**White Bread Flour**	3 cups
1 1/2 tsp.	**Dry Milk**	1/2 Tbsp.
1 Tbsp.	**Sugar**	2 Tbsp.
1/2 tsp.	**Salt**	1 tsp.
1/2 cup	**Pepper Jack Cheese**	3/4 cup
1/2 tsp.	**Red Peppers** *dried/crushed*	1 tsp.
2 tsp.	**Cilantro** *dried*	3 tsp.
1 tsp.	**Yeast** *fast rise*	2 tsp.
	- or -	
2 tsp.	**Yeast** *active dry*	3 tsp.

Remove dough from the machine after the dough or manual cycle is completed, then follow the process steps.

Turn dough onto lightly floured surface. Punch down and divide dough into 12 parts for large loaf, 8 parts for regular. Form each piece into a 7" rope and tie in knot. Place in greased muffin tin or on a cookie sheet and allow to rise for 25 minutes. Brush with egg, and bake at 375° for 20 - 25 minutes.

Picnic Basket

Calories 143
Cholesterol 0 mg.
Sodium 267 mg.
Protein 13 %
Carbohydrates 84 %
Fat 3 %

Nutritional information for 2 oz. serving without chicken

regular loaf		large loaf
3/4 cup +1 Tbsp.	**Water**	1 1/2 cups
2 cups	**White Bread Flour**	3 1/4 cups
1 Tbsp.	**Sugar**	1 1/2 Tbsp.
1 tsp.	**Salt**	1 1/2 tsp.
1 tsp.	**Yeast** fast rise	2 tsp.
	- or -	
1 1/2 tsp.	**Yeast** active dry	3 tsp.

Lynn's mother, Virginia Alexander, invented this ingenious dish years ago after her teenagers lost too many kitchen containers at the beach. With this oh-so-easy recipe, you bake your own basket - and then eat it!

Remove dough from the machine after the dough or manual cycle is completed, then follow the process steps.

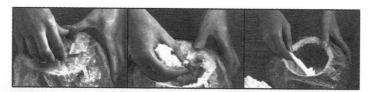

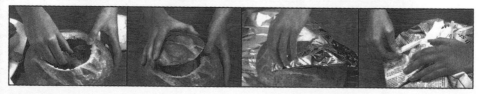

Turn dough out onto lightly floured surface, and carefully form into a ball without punching down. Place onto greased cookie sheet and let rise about one hour until double in size. Brush with beaten egg and bake at 375° for 25 - 35 minutes until golden brown. Let cool. Hollow out cooled bread like a pumpkin, reserving "lid" to put back on. Butter inside and fill with fried chicken. Replace lid and wrap in heavy duty foil, then newspaper, then foil again. Bread and chicken will stay warm all day. All you need is a sunny day, a few ants and some sand!

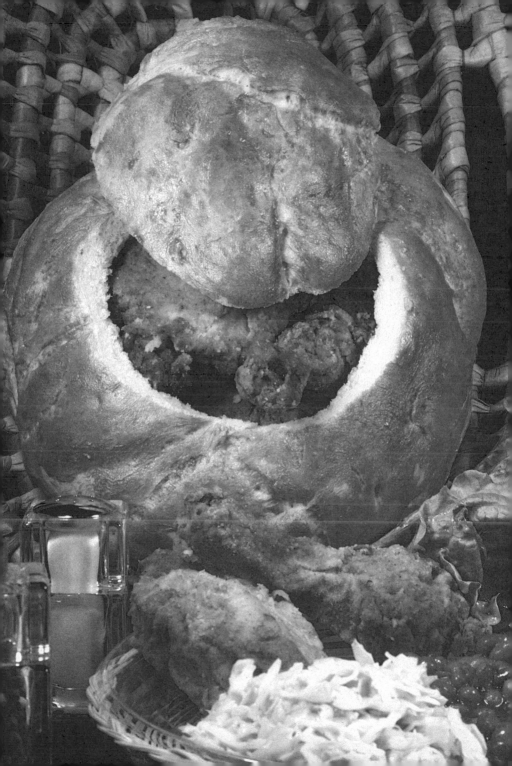

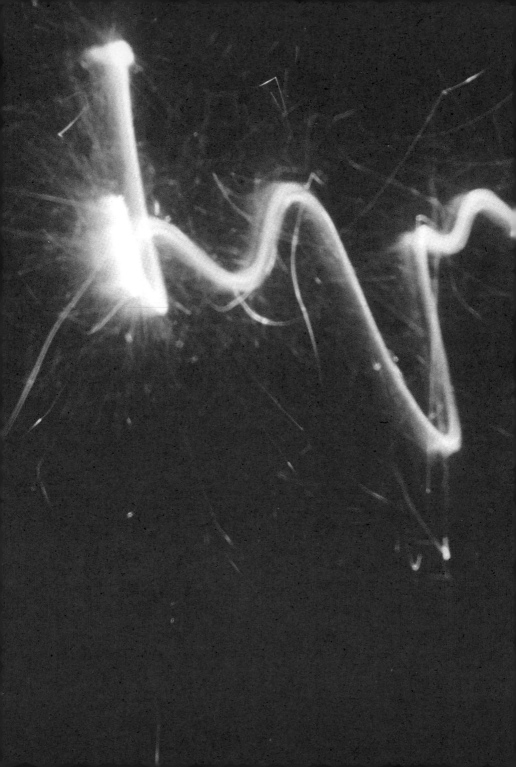

Unique Spreads, Troubleshooting & Accessories

Here's a trio of topics to help you get the most from your machine. Our sweet and savory spreads can enhance any bread - and they're so easy! The Troubleshooting section aims to help you avoid the most common mistakes. And our assortment of handy accessories make bread baking easier and more fun than ever.

SPREADS
Some are Savory......

Zippy Blue Cheese

3/4 C.   Crumbled Blue Cheese
1 C.   Creamed Cottage Cheese
1/2 C.   Butter or Margarine
1 tsp.   Fresh Basil
1 1/2 tsp.   Oregano Leaves
1 tsp.   Chili Powder
1/4 tsp.   Ground White Pepper

Blend together and store in refrigerator.

Lemon Mustard Butter

1/2 C.   Sweet Butter or Margarine
2 T.   Lemon Juice
1/2 tsp.   Grated Fresh Lemon Rind
1 1/2 T.   Dijon Mustard
Salt and Pepper to taste

Blend together and store in refrigerator.

Jezebel Jam

1/4 C.   Prepared Horseradish
12-oz Jar   Peach-Pineapple Jam
12-oz Jar   Apple Jelly
2 T.   Dry Mustard
1 T.   Ground White Pepper

Mix well and store in refrigerator.

Tarragon-Salmon Spread

1/2 C.   Canned Salmon
1/4 C.   Smoked Salmon
1/2 C.   Butter or Margarine
2 tsp.   Dried Tarragon
1/8 C.   Vodka
Salt and Pepper to taste

Blend together and store in refrigerator.

Chive Roquefort

1/4 C.   Cream Cheese
1/2 C.   Crumbled Roquefort
1/2 C.   Butter or Margarine
2 1/2 T.   Chopped Fresh Chives
1 T.   Lemon Juice
Salt and Pepper to taste

Blend together and store in refrigerator.

Curried Butter

1/2 C.   Butter or Margarine
3/4 tsp.   Curry Powder
1/8 tsp.   Paprika
Dash   Fresh Ground Pepper

Blend together and store in refrigerator.

Hot Chili & Garlic Butter

1/2 C.   Butter or Margarine
1 T.   Prepared Garlic
1 1/4 T.   Red Pepper Flakes
Salt to taste

Blend together and store in refrigerator.

Caraway Blue Cheese

1/3 C.   Crumbled Blue Cheese
3 oz.   Cream Cheese
1/3 C.   Mayonnaise
1 1/2 tsp.   Caraway Seed
White Pepper to taste

Blend together and store in refrigerator.

Green Peppercorn Butter

3 T.   Minced Shallots
3 T.   Butter
3 T.   Brandy
2 T.   Chopped Green Peppercorns
2 tsp.   Dijon Mustard
1/2 C.   Soft Butter or Margarine
1/4 C.   Sour Cream
1   Bouillon Cube (crushed)

Saute shallots in 3 T. butter until gold in color.
Add brandy and reduce by half on high heat.
Add bouillon, peppercorns, and mustard.
When cool mix with butter and cream. Store in refrigerator.

Some are Sweet........

Ginger-Pecan Butter

3/4 C.   Sweet Butter or Margarine
1/2 C.   Pecans, finely ground
2 T.   Ground Crystallized Ginger
1 tsp.   Brown Sugar
1/2 tsp. Allspice

Mix together and store in refrigerator.

Orange-Honey Butter

1 C.   Butter, softened
1/3 C. Honey
1 T.   Grated Fresh Orange Peel
1 T.   Orange Juice Frozen Concentrate

Blend together and store in refrigerator.

Guava-Raisin Spread

1 C.   Raisins
2/3 C.   Water
1 tsp.   Dry Mustard
1 1/2 T. Grated Fresh Orange Peel
1 C.   Guava Jelly

Boil raisins and water until water is absorbed, mixing well. Stir in other ingredients. Re-heat, mixing well. Cool then store in refrigerator.

Honey Butter

3/4 C.   Butter or Margarine
3/4 C.   Honey
3/4 C.   Powdered Sugar
1 tsp.   Cinnamon

Mix or blend together and store in refrigerator.

Brie Walnut Spread

3/4 C. Brie
1/2 C. Cream Cheese
2 T.   Kirsch Liqueur
1/2 C. Walnut Pieces

Blend cheeses and Kirsch together in food processor. Stir in nuts. Store in refrigerator.

Simple Chutney Cheese

1   8-oz. pkg. Cream Cheese
1 C. Apple Chutney
      Store bought

Mix together and store in refrigerator.

Cheesy Lemon

2   Eggs, slightly beaten
1/4 C. Lemon Juice
3 T.   Butter or Margarine
3/4 C. Sugar
1 tsp. Grated Fresh Lemon Peel
Dash   Salt
1   3-oz. pkg. Cream Cheese

In heavy pan mix eggs, juice, butter, sugar and salt. Bring to a boil while stirring over low heat, then cook 3 minutes more. Beat cream cheese and lemon peel. When egg mixture is cool, blend into cheese until smooth and store in refrigerator.

Paskha

2   Egg Yolks
1/2 C.   Raisins
1/4 C.   Rum
1/4 C.   Butter
1 C.   Powdered Sugar
1 tsp.   Vanilla
zest of 1 Lemon
1   6-oz. pkg Cream Cheese
1/2 C.   Toasted Almonds slivered

Soak raisins in rum overnight. Blend butter and cream cheese, add egg yolks, powdered sugar, lemon and vanilla. Fold in raisins, rum and almonds. Chill overnight.

Gruyere Apple Spread

1   6-oz. pkg. Cream Cheese
1 C.   Shredded Gruyere Cheese
1 T.   Milk
1 1/2 tsp. Prepared Mustard
1/2 C.   Shredded, Peeled Apple
1 1/2 tsp. Chopped Chives

Beat cream cheese, blend in gruyere, milk and mustard. Stir in remaining ingredients.

143

TROUBLESHOOTING

Okay, we admit it: in baking over 10,000 test loaves, we experienced a few failures. We've had our share of whole wheat door stops and pumpernickel hockey pucks. We've had loaves that caved in like the Grand Canyon, and loaves that exploded into mushrooms so airy we were tempted to tether them over the test kitchen like helium balloons.

But you know what? Those duds did not come from machine malfunction, the cause was usually human error.

Almost always, it came down to ingredients. Although bread machines are forgiving, they also are dependent on a consistent balance of ingredients. Loaves bomb out when that balance isn't maintained. Cheese, for instance, melts into liquid in the baking process, so a recipe with cheese generally needs less water. Adding raisins to a recipe can be half the fun - but you need to remember there's sugar in dried fruit, and possibly reduce your sugar accordingly.

The more you use your home bakery, the more you'll develop an instinct for the balance your particular machine requires with your chosen recipes, flours and yeasts. Remember, flour can vary from year to year as the weather and wheat crop change. Yeast is a living organism and occassionally a bottle may have more or less strength than usual.

Meanwhile, we'd like to share some other tips we picked up along the way. Some are little things like loading your dry ingredients outside the machine. For machines without removable buckets, we used (and reused) disposable tin pans. Measure the dry ingredients then fold and pour. Not only does it simplify measuring, loading the ingredients on your counter means you can avoid the cheap thrill of finding your machine smoking because spilled flour is burning under the pan.

On the following pages, we talk about gnarly loaves, pudding pockets, mushroom bread, and even dirty dancing.

Relax, this is easier than it sounds.

Right: These loaves were products of too much going on in our test kitchen at one time. Keeping a close eye on measurements will keep mistakes like these to a minimum.

CRATERED BREAD - If the top or sides cave in, you've probably got substantially too much moisture. Try reducing your water by 1/8 cup. . . If you're using canned fruit or vegetables, drain well and blot them dry . . . Try to remove your bread from its pan when baking is completed. Leaving a loaf in the pan can result in soggy sides and silly shapes. . .Sometimes craters occur when the yeast makes bread rise beyond the flour's ability to sustain the structure. Try adding a teaspoon of lemon juice to the recipe if you think the flour might be the cause. . .Crater loaves also happen with cheese breads; they taste great but getting the liquid content right can be tricky since each cheese has its own moisture content.

Controlled test bake using too much water.

PUDDING POCKETS - The center of this loaf isn't cooked all the way through. Typically it happens with heavier flours such as whole wheat, rye and bran. One solution is an extra knead. After the first knead, let the dough rise, then restart the machine at the very beginning as for a new loaf of bread. That puts more air into the dough. . . Another culprit may be moist ingredients such as yogurt, applesauce, canned chilies and canned fruit. Try reducing your liquids a tablespoon at a time.

MUSHROOM BREAD - There's too much yeast, it's blown its top, it's officially overproofed. Are you using the right yeast with the right measurement? Our recipes give two yeast measurements. *Use **either** active dry **or** fast rise - not both!* Did you use a tablespoon by accident? Yeast is almost always measured in teaspoons. . . You may have too much sugar, or ingredients with natural sugar like dried fruit. Older dried fruit has a higher sugar content. Decrease the sugar or honey accordingly. . . Another possibility is a smidge too much water. Try decreasing it by one tablespoon at a time. . .Occasionally, finely ground, softer flours require slightly less water or yeast than the harder, heavier flours. If you've checked all of the above, and a recipe still consistently explodes in your machine, try this: replace 1/4 of the total flour with whole wheat flour or add 1/4 teaspoon of fresh lemon juice to the recipe.

Controlled test bake using too much yeast and sugar.

GNARLY LOAVES - You know the kind - they look like gnarly tree bark. Your dough probably needs more moisture; when it's too dry, it can't knead properly. Try reducing flour 1/8 cup at a time or increasing liquids 1 tablespoon at a time until you hit the right balance for your machine, flour and yeast.

DIRTY DANCING - Heavier doughs and extended kneading times may make your machine vibrate on the counter. Be sure it's on a firm, level surface well away from the edge. It didn't happen to us, but we've heard of them dancing off the counter!

ROCKY MOUNTAIN HIGH - Live in a higher altitude? Your loaves may rise, look great - and then crash while baking. The low air pressure in higher altitudes means your yeast meets with less resistance, so your bread may make promises it can't keep; the bread can't sustain its own expansion. Experiment with reducing your yeast by 1/4 teaspoon at a time to slow the rising. Also try reducing water by no more than 1/8 cup. Our Colorado-based baker also solved this problem by also using a light, finely milled flour, which produced perfect loaves.

HOCKEY PUCKS - Some stone ground and whole wheat flours will bake a shorter loaf, but not a puck. If it looks like a hockey puck, you forgot your yeast. If the loaf is slightly higher, like a hockey puck on steroids, your yeast may be old. Test it by mixing one teaspoon of sugar and one tablespoon of yeast in one half cup of warm water. If the mixture doubles in volume in 15 minutes, the yeast is still good. . .Water that is either too hot or too cold is also a yeast inhibitor. Think tepid, like a baby's bath. . .Another possibility: accidentally measuring your salt with a tablespoon instead of a teaspoon.

Controlled test bake without yeast.

ON THE STREET WHERE YOU LIVE - Needless to say, summers in Anchorage, Alaska are different than summers in Albuquerque or Atlanta. Humidity, temperature, and water quality can effect your bread results. For instance, yeast may process faster in hot weather, so you may need less. In humid weather, heavier flours may absorb the moisture in the air more than finer, softer flours. We've told you what we discovered about the variables of flour, water and yeast, but you'll be the expert on *your* ingredients in *your* machine in *your* climate.

ACCESSORIES

ADJUSTABLE SPOONS AND SCOOP - Tired of juggling those little engraved measuring spoons like a charm bracelet to find the one you want? These adjustable spoons from KitchenArt not only end the juggling forever, they feature such hard to find measurements as 1/8, 1 1/2 and 2 1/2 teaspoons. And the new scoop measures 1/8 to 1/2 cup. Accurate and dishwasher safe. Scoop, $6.95; Spoon Set, $6.95.

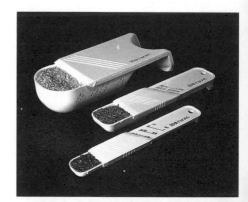

DRIED SPECIALTY FRUITS - Savor the taste of summer cherries and the tang of autumn cranberries all year long with Chukar brand dried fruits. Featured in our Chocolate Cherry, Tangy Cranberry, and Cherry Yogurt breads, they transform simple fruit bread into something *really* special. Both are a natural, chewy snack. 1 lb. bag of Cranberries, $8; or Cherries, $11

BREAD SAW AND CRUMB BOARD SETS - Created especially for *Electric Bread* by the Great American Toy Company in Seattle, this solid oak combination crumb and cutting board is designed to hold the largest machine loaves and catch all the crumbs. Appalachian Bow bread knife, in right and left-handed models, has a high carbon steel blade that slices even hot loaves! Choose an all oak set, oak with walnut, or oak with paduc. Crumb Board, $35; Bread Saw, $21; or the set, $50.

HEAVY DUTY, LIGHT WEIGHT -

These stylish, crystal clear canisters from Homelines look like glass, but they're actually feather-light acrylic. A large pail holds a 5 lb. bag of flour; buy one pail for white and one for whole wheat. Add the 4-piece canister set for sugar, salt, dry milk, and yeast, and you will have our 6-piece "Bread Baker's Bunch."

> Large Pail, $40;
> Two Pails, $70;
> Canister Set, $50;
> Baker's Bunch, $95.

HOT STUFF -

These unusual bread baskets from Vesture keep fresh baked bread warm using a unique gel pack. Heat the pack in your microwave and insert it into the special pouch in the basket's linen. Stays warm for up to three hours!
Regular Round Basket - $24.95;
Large Rectangular Basket - $29.95.

BREAD BUTCHER BLOCK CARTS -

Create a countertop for your bread machine with one of these handsome hard rock maple carts. The Open Shelf Cart features a spice rack, knife rack, pull-out bread board, towel bar and lots of storage to keep all your baking supplies together. The Cuisine Cart features a large drawer, solid back, towel bar and the tidiness of cupboard doors. These marvelous organizing stations are from Catskill Craftsman.

> Open Shelf Cart, $119.95;
> or the Cuisine Cart, $199.95.

Accessory Hotline
1-800-541-2733

149

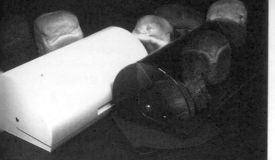

ASTONISHING ACRYLICS - These beautiful acrylic bread boxes by Emsa Frieling come in solid, creamy white or in the ebony with a clear front. Both are dishwasher safe with air ventilation engineered to extend bread freshness. $39.95.

EASY DOUGH - Here's two tools to simplify the tough tasks of cutting and rolling specialty doughs made in your bread machine. The wooden roller smoothly shapes the dough as desired. The easy-to-hold plastic cutter glides thru either dough or the finished product. The Cutter, available in black, white, green or red - $4; Roller - $6; or Both for $8.

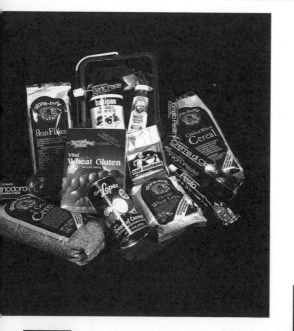

BASKET OF BOUNTY - Fascinated by our recipes, but can't find all the ingredients? Search no more! Our basket includes garlic, onion, pesto and tomato pastes, SAF and Bakipan yeasts, wheat gluten, coconut milk, wheat germ, cracked wheat, bran flakes, 7-Grain cereal and Cajun spice. Individual yeasts $5; other ingredients, $4; any three items for $10; or the entire Basket of Bounty $49.95.

Giving a gift? Send the Basket of Bounty with a copy of Electric Bread, $69.95.

JUMBO CROCK & SOURDOUGH - Strike it rich right there in your kitchen! This 7-cup capacity sourdough crock attractively stores the bubbling sourdough produced by our array of starters. The possibilities are endless for customizing your own breads. For starters, choose Mr. Baker's, $4; Tom's, $5; or Goldrush, $3; complete your selection with the large hand-crafted crock, $30.

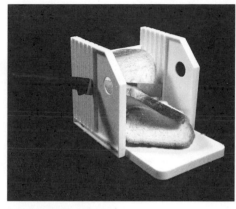

SIMPLE PERFECTION - Watching portions or making lots of sandwiches? This acrylic guide delivers an even slice of bread every time. $20.

FLOUR LEVELER - This is the best $1.50 you'll ever spend for accurately measured ingredients. This bowl scraper is perfect to level off your dry ingredients for a true measure.

LEATHER MITTS - Tired of dropping the pan when shaking out the loaf? Here's our test kitchen's solution. Imagine a soft, supple mitt with a firm grip, impervious to singes. Machine washable...we did, and it works! The mitts are available in hunter green, red, taupe, cobalt blue and black. $30 a pair.

ALASKAN SOURDOUGH KIT - If we could package the history, flavor and romance of the 49th state, this is how we'd do it. The starter has been passed down in Alaska since 1919, and was used by Ruth Allman, author of "Alaska Sourdough", the charming, anecdote-filled guide of an Alaskan pioneer. Since its arrival in our Anchorage test kitchen, Tom's hearty starter has produced flavorful bread machine loaves. The 2-cup jar hand crafted by Tom's Pots is the perfect size to refrigerate sourdough. Tom's Starter with a white, black or golden jar, $22; Ruth's Cookbook, $10; or the Alaskan Kit, $30.

FRESH SLICES - This new product from Farberware® combines bread storage with a convenient slicing tray that can also be used for serving. The canister keeps fresh bread airtight. Microwave, freezer and dishwasher safe - $15.

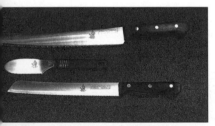

SLICING EASE - Messermeister bread knives, hand-crafted in Germany, are designed to glide through a hot loaf of bread. These handy knives will give you years of slicing ease. We've chosen three sizes: 10" Bread Knife, $32; 8" Bread Knife, $21; and the small Breakfast Knife, $5.50.

CLEARLY CORRECT - At our request, our friends at Emsa Frieling created the "Perfect Beaker" for liquid measurement. Uniquely shaped, the two cup capacity beaker is designed with lots of markings to ensure accuracy - cups, tablespoons, teaspoons, even metric! You'll love this easy-to-see measuring experience. Originally $7.95, now only $6.00.

CONTEMPORARY MEASURES -
Stylish but sturdy, this set of measuring cups and spoons is accurate, dishwasher safe, and available in either black or white with easy-to-read markings. Measuring cups and spoons, $10 for the set.

Accessory
Hotline
1-800-541-2733

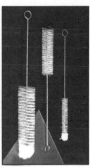

FOR A CLEAN MACHINE - Cleaning your bread machine has never been so easy. These Phoenixware brushes have handles long enough to reach anywhere in your machine, soft tips to prevent abrasions. Set of 3 brushes, $7.

The Mini Attachments turn your vacuum hose into a miniature powerhouse with flexible tubing, crevice and brush tools. Great for typewriters and computers, too! $13.

FIDDLE BOW KNIFE AND CRUMB TRAY - If anything harks back to hearth and home as much as home-made bread, it's fine woodworking. The cherry wood board with crumb tray elegantly catches the crumbs as the matching fiddle bow's serrated edge creates a perfect slice of hot bread. The crumb tray features a removable trivet with white acrylic interior for easy cleaning. Crumb tray, $39.95; Fiddle bow knife, $19.95; or buy the set for $54.95.

A Floral Vision
Action Graphics
Aluminum Housewares
American Leathers
Bromar Alaska
Catskill Craftsmen, Inc.
Charlescraft
Circulair
ColorArt Printing
ComputerLand
Conagra Grocery Products
Covenant House

CPC Specialty Products
Curtis & Campbell
DAMCO
Decosonic
Design Craft, Ltd.
Design Ideas
Dimond Graphics
Five Roses Flour
Frye International
Frieling USA, Inc.
Goldstar
HPA
Habitat
Haupt Enterprises

Hill Design
Hodgson Mill
Homelines International
King Arthur Flours
Laurel Group
Magic Seasoning Blends
Monogram Magic
Morton & Basset Spices
Mountain Woods
Natural Pantry
OXO International
Phoenixware
Salton Maxim
Singer
The Bakertowne, Inc.
The Computer Store
TimeFrame
Tom's Pots

Special Thanks

American Harvest
Arrowhead Mills
Bakipan
Black & Decker
Breadman
Chukar Cherries
Fleischmann's Yeast
Gold Medal-General Mills
Hitachi
MK Overseas
Panasonic Company
Pillsbury
Red Star Yeast
Regal Ware
Robin Hood-Multifoods
SAF Products Corporation
Sanyo-Fisher USA
Spice Islands
Stone-Buhr Flours
Sunbeam-Oster
Toastmaster
Welbilt Appliance Company
West Bend
Zojirushi American Corporation

Thanks to Bean's Cafe and
Catholic Social Services for
helping find homes for
over 10,000 loaves of bread.

Cindy Alexander
Don Alexander
Virginia Alexander
Dennis Aron
Malinda Aron
Sandy Asbell
Pam Auld
Barbara Bach
Tom Barnett
John Bevan
Lucy Bowman
Dennis Brandon
Milqueya Brekhus
Dale Campbell
Debbie Campbell
Mary Campbell
Maggie Carey
Dick Carpenter
Mikeil Carroll
Paul Cates
Betty Crews
Lorelle Delmotto

Paul Dodroe
Bernd Dressler
Don Edwards
John Ellenberger
Paula Etchison
Deanna Ferris
Frank Flavin
Boyd Foster
Bud Frye
Vicky Gayhano
Gary Glick
Carl Haggar
Bob Hebner
Augusto Hernandez
John Holliday
Tom Hughes
Bob Johnson
Masayoshi Kagita
Bob Kaufman
Arvid King
Steven King
Tom Lacalamita
Dave Lackey

Anita Lee
Gary Lindsey
Jim MacKay
Doug Marx
Mary Ann McCoy
Katie McElroy
John McKay
Chuck McMahon
Tom Meyers
Bud Morgan
Lynn Muckerheide
John Naylor
Ben Nomoto
Ken Normura
Cliff Olson
Pat Olson
Al Parrish
Vova Pavlenko
Margaret Price
Diane Quicksilver
Cathy Rasmuson
Jeffrey Riegel
Rabbi Harry Rosenfeld
Samaria Ross

Gretchen Sagan
Carina Saunders
Bernard Schnacke
Paul Schutt
Bill Sheffield
Bob Sisco
Reg Stranks
Cristanne Swanda
Chris Swalling
Cari Symonds
Miles Symonds
Andy Tanaka
Jil Thompson
Norman Thompson
Wanda Thompson
Laura Tilly
Mark Urdahl
Glenna Vance
Jerry Vandergriff
Cal Walters
Bill Weekly
Bonnie Welsh
Barbara Westfield

David Willis
Eva Willis
Marilyn Willis
Shirley Willis
V.B. Willis
Virlyn Willis
Bill Wilmot
Allyn Wilson
Connie Yoshimura
Phil Zarro
Barbara Zipkin
Z.J. Loussac Library
  Telephone Reference
  Librarians

ACKNOWLEDGEMENTS

Test Kitchen Team

Tim Doebler, C.W.C., C.C.E.
Greg Forte, C.E.C., C.C.E.
Executive Chef

Katy Middleton
Research

Lynn Brandon
Mary Ann Swalling
Test Kitchen Managers

Lara Parrish
Special Projects

- Technicians -

Jennifer Brandon
Victoria Carter
Kelli Deens
Cindy McMahon
Sue Anne Merrill
Diana Seropian
Sarah Strange
Elsie St. Regis
Mary J. Willis
Rebecca Zanin

Technical Assistance

Barbara Baugh
Colorprint International Co.
Helix
Helen Ide
Bruce Kiessling
Lanrie Leung
Eric Nancarrow
Christina Olson
Tennys Owens
Photowright
Marie Reisinger

Management

Ann Parrish
Mary Willis Kiessling
Millie Edwards
Shirley Laird

INDEX